Determining
Medical Fitness
to Operate Motor Vehicles

CMA Driver's Guide
7th edition

ASSOCIATION MÉDICALE CANADIENNE

CANADIAN MEDICAL ASSOCIATION

Published by the Canadian Medical Association

Library and Archives Canada Cataloguing in Publication

Determining medical fitness to operate motor vehicles : CMA driver's guide. -- 7th ed.

Issued also in French under title: Évaluation médicale de l'aptitude à conduire.

Includes index.

ISBN 1-894391-24-1

1. Automobile driving--Physiological aspects--Handbooks, manuals, etc.

2. Automobile drivers--Medical examinations--Handbooks, manuals, etc.

3. Automotive medicine--Handbooks, manuals, etc. I. Canadian Medical Association

TL152.35.D47 2006   629.28'302461   C2006-905040-6

Disclaimer: This guide is not a substitute for medical diagnosis, and readers are encouraged to use their best clinical judgement to determine a patient's medical fitness to drive. The naming of any organization, product or alternative therapy in this book does not imply endorsement by the Canadian Medical Association, nor does the omission of any such name imply disapproval by the Canadian Medical Association. The Canadian Medical Association does not assume any responsibility for liability arising from any error in or omission from the book, or from the use of any information contained in it.

Ordering information and additional copies are available from

Member Service Centre
Canadian Medical Association
1867 Alta Vista Dr.
Ottawa ON K1G 3Y6
888 855-2555 or 613 731-8610 x2307; fax 613 236-8864
cmamsc@cma.ca

Également disponible en français.

This document is available electronically at cma.ca

Contents

Acknowledgements

Scientific Editorial Board

Dr. David Butcher, Editor in Chief

Dr. Jamie Dow, Canadian Council of Motor Transport Administrators (liaison)

Dr. Ian G. Gillespie, Victoria, British Columbia

Dr. David W. Irving, Edmonton, Alberta

Dr. Malcolm Man-Son-Hing, Ottawa, Ontario

Dr. Christopher Simpson, Kingston, Ontario

Dr. Cathy Younger-Lewis, Consultant Editor

Contributing authors

Dr. Duncan Anderson (Vision)

Dr. William J. Beilby, Canadian Medical Protective Association (Reporting — When and why, App. A)

Dr. Dan Bergeron (Vision)

Dr. David Bowering (Introduction)

Dr. Edward Brook (Aviation)

Dr. David Butcher (Introduction)

Dr. Anne Cranney (Musculoskeletal disabilities)

Dr. John Cutbill (Railway)

Dr. Bonnie Dobbs (Driving cessation)

Dr. Jamie Dow (Functional assessment – emerging emphasis, Anesthesia and surgery, Seat belts and air bags, Motorcycles and off-road vehicles)

Dr. Nady el Guebaly (Alcohol, Drugs)

Dr. Hillel Finestone (Cerebrovascular diseases (including stroke) and traumatic brain injury, General debility)

Dr. Charles George (Sleep disorders)

Dr. Ian G. Gillespie (Psychiatric illness, Traumatic brain injury)

Dr. Roger Goldstein (Respiratory diseases)

Dr. Raju Hajela (Alcohol, Drugs)

Ms. Melody-Ann Isinger (Introduction)

Dr. Claude Lapierre (Railway)

Dr. Thomas Lindsay (Vascular diseases)

Dr. Malcolm Man-Son-Hing (Aging)

Ms. Wendy Nieuwland (Cerebrovascular diseases (including stroke) and traumatic brain injury)

Ms. Siobhan O'Donnell (Musculoskeletal disabilities)

Dr. Hugh O'Neill (Aviation)

Dr. Lorne Parnes (Auditory – vestibular disorders)

Dr. Guy Rémillard (Nervous system)

Dr. Cindy Jo Richardson (Endocrine and metabolic disorders)

Dr. Sabin Shurraw (Renal diseases)

Dr. Chris Simpson (Cardiovascular diseases)

Dr. Jacques Tittley (Vascular diseases)

Dr. Marcello Tonelli (Renal diseases)

Dr. Vincent Woo (Endocrine and metabolic disorders)

Dr. Benjamin Zifkin (Nervous system)

CMA staff

Dr. Isra G. Levy, Chief Medical Officer and editorial liaison

Ms. Ann Chénier, Editorial Administrator

Ms. Jean Nelson, Legal Consultant

Mr. Akhilesh Patel, Research Assistant

Ms. Carol Rochefort, Managing Editor

Ms. Debbie Rupert, Manager, Publishing Services

Ms. Sharon Vanin, Legal Consultant

Consultation responses

Alberta Medical Association

British Columbia Ministry of Public Safety and Solicitor General, Office of the Superintendent of Motor Vehicles

Canadian Anesthesiologists' Society

Canadian Association of Optometrists

Canadian Association of Physical Medicine and Rehabilitation

Canadian Medical Protective Association

Canadian Ophthalmological Society

Canadian Physiotherapy Association

Canadian Psychological Association

CanDRIVE

Dr. Bonnie Cham, Chair, CMA Committee on Ethics

Dr. Laurence Jerome, Adjunct Professor of Psychiatry, the University of Western Ontario

Dr. Alvin U. Segal, The University of Western Ontario

Dr. Colin McMillan, Chair, CMA Board of Directors

Dr. James Silvius, Member, CMA Council on Health Care and Promotion

Dr. Michael Sharma, The Ottawa Hospital

Driver Fitness and Monitoring Branch, Infrastructure and Transportation, Alberta

Federation of Medical Women of Canada

Manitoba Public Insurance

Medical Review Unit, SGI, Saskatchewan

Medical Society of Prince Edward Island

New Brunswick Department of Public Safety, Motor Vehicle Branch

Ontario Driver Improvement Office, Ministry of Transportation

Society of Rural Physicians of Canada

Section 1
Introduction

1.1 Changes to the guide

The Canadian Medical Association (CMA) has prepared this guide to help physicians determine whether their patients are medically fit to drive a motor vehicle safely. This 7th edition is designed to serve as a handy office resource and user-friendly tool for physicians. Existing sections on various medical conditions have been updated extensively and new sections — such as "driving cessation" and "functional assessment" — have been added. The medico–legal section has been revised with a focus on reporting, and a new appendix from the Canadian Medical Protective Association (Appendix A) has been included.

Each section now includes an "alert box" highlighting key information in the section. This is to help physicians who may have to make immediate decisions about a patient's fitness to drive, often in a clinical situation not directly related to driving. The book's index and subheadings have been designed to help physicians quickly find the discussion of relevant medical conditions as they assess their patients. The appendices contain tools for evaluating alcohol (Appendix B and C) and dementia illnesses (Appendix D) as well as contact names and numbers for the provincial and territorial ministries of transportation (Appendix E).

Also new to the guide are sections on assessing medical fitness for railway and aviation workers. These sections include a summary of the regulatory framework governing railway workers and pilots, along with a discussion of functional assessment for different categories of workers with reference to comparable classes of driver's licences and the identification of standards that are specific or unique to these industries. These sections include contact information for reporting potentially unfit railway workers and pilots. Maritime workers are not included, as currently there are no federally mandated medical fitness standards for these workers.

1.2 Functional assessment

Since the 6th edition of this guide was published, a landmark legal ruling[*] identified the right of Canadian drivers to have their licence eligibility determined based on an individ-

---

[*]British Columbia (Superintendent of Motor Vehicles) v. British Columbia (Council of Human Rights), [1999] 3 S.C.R. 868. Available at scc.lexum.umontreal.ca/en/1999/1999rcs3-868/1999rcs3-868.html (accessed 24 Aug. 2006).

ual functional assessment, rather than exclusively on a diagnosis, with a corresponding responsibility for licensing authorities to accommodate drivers wherever possible within safe limits. This can often be achieved with appropriate licence conditions or restrictions or vehicle modifications, which may be based on a physician's recommendation. Physicians should be aware of the need to review their patients' medical fitness to drive based on an assessment of their overall functional capacity, including their ability to accommodate to medical and physical deficits. Physicians should also consider the impact of multiple medical conditions, as well as aging or other circumstances, on their patients' overall functional capacity and fitness to drive.

Many drivers have chronic medical conditions that have the potential to impair their fitness to drive. For these drivers, the level of knowledge of and insight into their medical condition, along with their ability to self-manage the condition, compliance with physician-prescribed treatment and ability to modify their driving activities to accommodate their condition should form a basis for physician assessment of their fitness to drive.

This edition has a new section (section 4, Driving cessation) that addresses these issues.

Physicians may refer their patients for an assessment of their fitness to drive. Driver assessment is multifactorial and may include a road test with a driver examiner. A road test alone may be indicated in some circumstances to assess individual capability to adapt to a physical or medical disability, but it is not the same as a functional driver assessment. Physicians can locate a driver assessment centre by contacting the provincial or territorial ministry of transportation in their jurisdiction (see Appendix E).

1.3   Medical standards for fitness to drive

Many of the recommendations in this guide are the same as the standards found in such documents as the Canadian Council of Motor Transport Administrators' (CCMTA) Medical Standards for Drivers (formerly called the National Safety Code). The CCMTA publication was developed in meetings of the medical consultants from each province and territory who are responsible for advising the motor vehicle licensing authorities on medical matters and safety in driving. These medical standards are revised annually by the Medical Advisory Committee of the CCMTA, and the majority are adopted by the provincial and territorial motor vehicle licensing departments. This achieves a uniformity of standards across Canada with the result that a driver licensed in one province or territory is considered licensed in all other provinces and territories.

To minimize impediments to commercial drivers who must cross the Canada–United States border, an agreement has been reached whereby each country recognizes the medical standards of the other. The only exceptions concern insulin-treated diabetes, epilepsy and hearing deficits. Canadian commercial drivers with these conditions cannot cross the border to the United States with their commercial vehicle. Private drivers and commercial drivers who are driving a private vehicle are not affected by this measure.

1.4   Methods

To produce this edition, the CMA undertook an evidence-based review of medical standards under the leadership of a Scientific Editorial Board, comprising 5 member physicians and an editor-in-chief with a range of relevant practice and advisory experience pertaining to driver fitness and safety. Starting with the 2000 6th edition, the editorial board produced a draft for this new edition. Some sections were written or edited by selected physicians with expertise in the clinical field, while others reflect consensus documents from specialty societies (notably the Canadian Cardiovascular Society and the Canadian Ophthalmological Society). The draft was widely circulated to medical and non-medical organizations, provincial driving authorities and selected experts. All comments were considered by the Scientific Editorial Board.

Although there is still comparatively little scientific evidence available to assess the degree of impairment to driving that results from most medical disabilities, the evidence is increasing. The Scientific Editorial Board was aided in the preparation of this guide by a review of recent scientific reports for each section.* In addition, a "risk of harm" formula (Appendix F) is introduced to support the Canadian Cardiovascular Society recommendations on fitness to drive (section 13). However, the recommendations remain mainly empirical and reflect the fact that the driving standards are based on the consensus opinion of an expert panel supported by a careful review of the pertinent research, examination of international and national standards and consensus, as well as the collected experience of a number of specialists in the area. They are intended to impose no more than common sense restrictions on drivers with medical disabilities. This guide is not a collection of hard-and-fast rules; nor does it have the force of law.

1.5   The physician's role

Every physician who examines a patient to determine fitness to drive must always consider both the interest of the patient and the welfare of the community exposed to the patient's driving. In the course of the examination, the physician should not only look for physical disabilities but also endeavour to assess the patient's mental and emotional fitness to drive safely. A single major impairment or multiple minor functional defects may make it unsafe

---

*Interested readers are referred to a study undertaken by Monash University Accident Research Centre, the most complete and detailed review of the evidence supporting medical standards for drivers at the time of writing of this guide. See Charlton JL, Koppel S, O'Hare M, et al. *Influence of chronic illness on crash involvement of motor vehicle drivers.* Victoria, Australia: Monash University Accident Research Centre; 2004. Available at: www.monash.edu.au/muarc/reports/muarc213.html (accessed 23 Aug 2006).

for the person to drive. Likewise, physicians should be aware of their responsibility or legislated requirement to report patients with medical conditions that make it unsafe for them to drive, according to the jurisdiction in which they practise. The physician should also be aware of the circumstances in which patients will likely function. For example, the extreme demands related to operating police and emergency vehicles suggest that drivers of these vehicles should be cautioned that even relatively minor functional defects may make it unsafe for them to drive.

1.6   Public health

Motor vehicle crashes kill about 3000 people in Canada each year and injure another 250 000. By contrast, the number of deaths attributable to SARS in 2003 was 44 and the number of deaths from West Nile Virus in 2005 was 24.

Most motor vehicle crashes involve people between the ages of 15 and 55 years. Crashes are a leading cause of death and disability in these age groups. Major contributing factors to crashes in younger people are alcohol, speeding and poor judgement, including driving inappropriately for weather and road conditions and failure to use safety equipment. Also, when driving exposure is taken into account, drivers over the age of 75 have much higher than average crash rates. In older people, the primary reason for crashes is the development of medical conditions that affect fitness to drive. Private drivers increasingly share the roads with commercial drivers and almost half of the crashes that occur involve at least one commercial vehicle.

Anything that physicians can do to encourage safe driving by their patients has a positive public health impact. Questions regarding drinking and driving and seat belt use should be considered to be at least as important as questions regarding smoking behaviour. The prevention of motor vehicle crashes has at least as great an impact on population health as trauma programs that treat crash victims. The health of commercial drivers is also an important consideration given their long hours on the road and their vulnerability to metabolic disease, fatigue and stimulant use. It is imperative that physicians understand the increased risks associated with obstructive sleep apnea, cardiovascular diseases, addictions and other conditions that may reduce driver fitness.

1.7   Levels of medical fitness required by the motor vehicle licensing authorities

The motor vehicle licensing authorities have the power to issue and suspend licences. Legislation in the provincial and territorial jurisdictions stipulates that these authorities can require licensed drivers to be examined for their fitness to drive. "Fitness" is considered to mean fitness in the medical sense. The provincial motor vehicle licensing authorities have the final responsibility for determining licence eligibility, and fitness to drive is a major determinant of eligibility. The recommendations of the CMA outlined in this guide are meant to assist physicians in determining whether a person is medically fit and to identify conditions that will likely disqualify a person from holding a licence.

The classification of drivers' licences does not take into account the context of driving activities, nor do licensing authorities regulate driving activity. However, the amount driven and the environment in which driving takes place are important predictors of risk. This guide refers to "private" and "commercial" drivers with varying recommended standards of fitness. Drivers of vehicles for which a Class 5 licence is applicable may be considered to be commercial drivers based on the amount driven. Physicians should assess their patients for fitness to drive in the context in which they will be driving and advise them accordingly.

The motor vehicle licensing authorities require a higher level of fitness of commercial drivers who operate passenger-carrying vehicles, trucks and emergency vehicles. These drivers spend many more hours at the wheel, often under far more adverse driving conditions, than private vehicle drivers. Commercial drivers are usually unable to select their hours of work and cannot readily abandon their passengers or cargo should they become unwell while on duty. Commercial drivers may also be called on to undertake heavy physical work, such as loading or unloading their vehicles, realigning shifted loads and putting on and removing chains. In addition, should the commercial driver suffer a collision, the consequences are much more likely to be serious, particularly when the driver is carrying passengers or dangerous cargo. People operating emergency vehicles are frequently required to drive under considerable stress because of the nature of their work. Inclement weather, when driving conditions are less than ideal, is often a factor. This group should also be expected to meet higher medical standards than private drivers.

Physicians should be aware that the medical standards of fitness and criteria for licensure for drivers of motor vehicles are not necessarily the same as those for pilots and railway workers. Medical conditions that are not of concern with respect to driving may be considered disabling for pilots or railway workers. The physical demands of the activity and the ability to stop if unwell vary between the various modes of transport leading to different assessments of the risk created by medical conditions.

1.8   Driver's medical examination report

If, after completing a driver's medical examination, a physician is undecided about a patient's fitness to drive, the physician should consider arranging for a consultation with an appropriate specialist. A copy of the specialist's report should accompany the medical form when it is returned to the motor vehicle licensing authority. Alternatively, physicians may consider referring a patient to a driver assessment centre if a functional assessment is beyond the scope of the examining physician.

A medical examination is mandatory for some classes of licences. The licensing authority may base a final decision regarding a driver's licence eligibility on the examining physician's opinion. Where no opinion is given or where the information in the report differs significantly from previous reports submitted by other physicians or conflicts with statements made by the driver, the motor vehicle licensing authority will often ask its own medical consultants for a recommendation.

1.9 Payment for medical and laboratory examinations

In some jurisdictions, patients are responsible for paying for all medical reports and laboratory examinations carried out for the purpose of obtaining or retaining a driver's licence, even though these examinations or tests may have been requested by the motor vehicle licensing authority. In other provinces, examinations for some drivers, such as seniors, are insured services or it is the responsibility of the employers of the drivers to cover such costs.

1.10 Classes of drivers' licences and vehicles

Drivers' licences are divided into classes according to the types of motor vehicles the holder is permitted to drive. **The classifications can vary across jurisdictions, and graduated licensing systems have been instituted in some jurisdictions. In this guide, therefore, licences and vehicles are classified generically, and readers should refer to the provincial or territorial classification when necessary** (see Appendix E for contact information).

Class 1: Permits the operation of a motor vehicle of any type or size, with or without passengers, and a trailer of any size.

Class 2: Permits the operation of a motor vehicle of any type or size, with or without passengers. A Class 2 licence does not permit the holder to pull a semi-trailer.

Class 3: Permits the operation of a motor vehicle of any size. A Class 3 licence does not permit the holder to carry passengers or to pull a semi-trailer.

Class 4: Permits the operation of a taxicab, a bus carrying no more than 24 passengers and emergency response vehicles, such as ambulances, fire trucks and police cars.

Class 5: Permits the operation of any motor vehicle or small truck (a towed vehicle cannot exceed 4600 kg). A Class 5 licence does not permit the holder to drive an ambulance, a taxicab or a bus or to pull a semi-trailer.

Class 6: Permits the operation of a motorcycle, motor scooter or minibike only. All other classes must be endorsed to include Class 6 before the holder may operate a motorcycle, motor scooter or minibike.

1.11   Contact us

Physicians who have comments and suggestions about the guide's recommendations are invited to contact the Canadian Medical Association, 1867 Alta Vista Drive, Ottawa ON K1G 3Y6, by email at: cmamsc@cma.ca.

Section 2
Functional assessment — emerging emphasis

Alert box

Medical standards for drivers often cannot be applied without considering the functional impact of the medical condition on the individual.

All Canadian jurisdictions have policies in place that allow individuals the opportunity to demonstrate that they are capable of driving safely despite the limitations implied by a diagnosis. Criteria may vary among jurisdictions.

2.1   Overview

Historically, determining medical fitness to drive was based solely on a medical office examination and a diagnosis. However, recent court decisions recognize that the ability of a driver to accommodate and function with a given medical condition varies with the individual. These court decisions have also established the right of individuals to be assessed individually for their ability to drive safely. A functional assessment, which is a structured assessment of the individual's ability to perform the actions and exercise the judgement necessary for safe driving — and often includes a road test — takes this individual variation into account. Functional assessments may be available only in urban centres and may be difficult to arrange for patients in rural areas.

A driver with a medical condition that can compromise cognitive or motor skills may require a functional assessment to determine fitness to drive. Any compromise of the ability to perform daily activities should trigger some sort of functional driving assessment.

2.2   Standards

Canadian jurisdictions are working to develop and apply standards that permit individual assessment of functional capabilities of drivers with medical conditions that may affect driving.

Medical standards for drivers must address three different types of conditions:

Functional limitations: Certain medical conditions, or combination of medical conditions, can lead to limitations of functional capabilities (e.g., the amputation of a foot will have an impact on the ability to drive with a manual transmission).

Associated risk: The risk of a catastrophic event due to a medical condition may be judged to be unacceptable. Certain heart conditions are examples of medical conditions where the risk of an incapacitating event occurring while driving has led to the definition of criteria designed to diminish the risk.

Use of substances judged incompatible with driving: Illicit drugs, alcohol and medications may interfere with fitness to drive.

2.3   Assessment

2.3.1   *Office assessment*

Physicians in a medical office setting can assess their patients' fitness to drive when the patients are clearly either capable or incapable of driving. This guide provides information to assist with those decisions. In less clear-cut situations, it may be necessary for the physician to employ other means of testing to perform a functional assessment. This usually involves on-road testing.

It should be emphasized that, with the exception of temporary restrictions for short-term medical situations, the physician is not required to determine whether a licence will be granted or suspended. The physician's responsibility is to describe the situation, and the licensing agency will make a decision based on the physician's observations and its interpretation of the regulations.

2.3.2   *Functional assessment*

A functional assessment is appropriate when the medical condition in question is present all of the time. Functional assessment is not appropriate when the driver has a medical condition that is episodic (e.g., seizures) and known to be associated with increased risk.

Licensing authorities make their own decisions about the evidence and opinions on which to base their decision. There is a role for specialized road testing and computerized screening, as well as some self-administered tests (as long as the patient has insight). Physicians may choose to refer a patient for additional assessment when such resources are available to their patients. The decision to refer for assessment can be deferred to the licensing authority. Assessments are usually available through private companies and are paid for by the driver (see Appendix E). Some public health care facilities offer driving assessments free of charge, but access is limited and waiting lists tend to be long.

Some jurisdictions use off-road evaluations, such as driving simulators or batteries of tests to predict on-road behaviour. Computerized testing may provide useful objective information about functions believed to be important for safe driving. However, there is insufficient evidence either to support or refute making licensing decisions based solely on their results.

Most Canadian jurisdictions have some form of formal road testing in place, often conducted by occupational therapists specialized in the functional testing of drivers. In some jurisdictions, certified technicians do the testing. Assessments are normally limited to drivers of private cars. Drivers of commercial vehicles and motorcycles usually cannot be evaluated in private centres.

Currently, there is insufficient evidence to recommend for or against any specific testing method. Authoritative research in this field demonstrates clearly that the novice driver's road test is inappropriate for experienced drivers. Ideally, the experienced driver's test should take place in surroundings familiar to the driver and, if possible, in his or her own car. Safety considerations and distance may preclude this, which makes standardized testing difficult.

Section 3
Reporting — when and why*

Alert box

Physicians have a statutory duty to report patients whom they believe to be unfit to drive to the relevant provincial or territorial motor vehicle licensing authority. This duty may be mandatory or discretionary, depending on the province or territory involved. This duty to report is owed to the public and supersedes the physician's private duty with regard to confidentiality

3.1   Overview

All provinces and territories impose a statutory duty on physicians relating to the reporting of patients deemed unfit to drive. This duty may be mandatory or discretionary, depending on the jurisdiction (see Table 1).† The duty to report prevails over a physician's duty of confidentiality. Section 35 of the CMA *Code of Ethics* affirms the notion that physician-patient confidentiality may be breached when required or permitted by law:

Disclose your patients' personal health information to third parties only with their consent, or as provided for by law, such as when the maintenance of confidentiality would result in a significant risk of substantial harm to others or, in the case of incompetent patients, to the patients themselves. In such cases, take all reasonable steps to inform the patients that the usual requirements for confidentiality will be breached.

Despite being legally authorized to breach confidentiality in these circumstances, physicians often find it difficult to report patients who are deemed unfit to drive. Physicians are often concerned about their own liability and, particularly when the patient is a commercial driver, are concerned about the impact of a suspension or restriction of licence on the patient.

---

*This section is meant for educational purposes as a guide to physicians on reporting of patients assessed to be unfit to drive. It is not meant to replace legal counsel. Unless specified, this section refers to fitness to drive motor vehicles.

†Pilots, air traffic controllers and certain designated railway workers are governed by federal legislation that requires the reporting of certain individuals in these transportation industries who have a medical condition rendering them unfit to perform their duties. These reporting obligations are discussed in separate sections of this guide.

Physicians also may have difficulty determining the circumstances in which a report should be made. Reference to this guide, to the specific wording of the relevant legislation and to the Canadian Medical Protective Association (CMPA) is helpful in these circumstances.

It is important to emphasize that only motor vehicle licensing authorities can suspend or restrict a person's licence. While a physician's report is a very important element in determining the motor vehicle licensing authority's subsequent action, it is not the physician's responsibility to determine whether the patient's driving privileges should be altered.

Physicians should also be aware that in all jurisdictions, the relevant legislation protects the physician from any legal action brought against the physician for making a report (see Table 1). Some provinces and territories specify that the physician must have acted in good faith in order to benefit from this protection.

Physicians should be aware that there have been cases where injured parties in a motor vehicle crash have brought actions against physicians, alleging that the crash was caused in part by the medical disability of their patient, who should not have been allowed to continue driving. Physicians have been found liable for failing to report, notably in those provinces and territories with mandatory requirements.

It is, therefore, important for physicians to fulfill their statutory duties and report patients whom they believe have a medical condition that might reasonably make it dangerous for them to drive. Physicians are encouraged to be familiar with this guide when assessing a patient's fitness to drive and when deciding whether to report a particular patient.

3.2   Reporting

Physicians who have determined that a patient is unfit to drive should inform the patient that a report will be made to the motor vehicle licensing authority and they should document this discussion in the patient's medical chart. In general, physicians should err on the side of reporting any potentially medically unfit driver. This is especially important in jurisdictions where there is a mandatory reporting obligation. Contact your provincial or territorial motor vehicle licensing authority for details on the process for reporting in your jurisdiction, or for advice on interpreting jurisdictional standards (see Appendix E).

3.3   Patient's right of access to physician's report

The right of patients to access reports about fitness to drive made to the motor vehicle licensing authority and any notes made in the medical chart about such a report is subject to varying legislation in the provinces and territories. Physicians should contact the CMPA for further information specific to their jurisdiction.

Table 1: Regulations governing reporting of medically unfit drivers and protection for physicians

Jurisdiction	Reporting	MD protection for reporting	Admissibility of reports as evidence in legal proceedings
Alberta	Not directly addressed, but interpreted as discretionary	Protected	Reports confidential
British Columbia	Mandatory for MD if the unfit driver has been warned of the danger and still continues to drive	Protected unless physician acts falsely or maliciously	Not addressed Subject to the provisions of access to information legislation
Manitoba	Mandatory	Protected	Privileged Not admissible as evidence except to prove compliance with reporting obligations
New Brunswick	Mandatory	Protected as long as physician acts in good faith	Not addressed
Newfoundland and Labrador	Mandatory	Protected	Privileged Not admissible in evidence in trial except to prove compliance with reporting obligations
Northwest Territories	Mandatory	Protected unless physician acts maliciously or without reasonable grounds	Not admissible in evidence or open to public inspection except to prove compliance with the reporting provision and in a prosecution of a contravention of section 330 (making false statements or submitting false documents). The person who is the subject of the report is entitled to a copy of the report upon payment of a prescribed fee.
Nova Scotia	Discretionary	Protected	Not addressed Subject to access to information legislation
Nunavut	Mandatory	Protected unless physician acts maliciously or without reasonable grounds	Not admissible in evidence or open to public inspection except to prove compliance with the reporting provision and in a prosecution of a contravention of section 330 (making false statements or submitting false documents). The person who is the subject of the report is entitled to a copy of the report upon payment of a prescribed fee.
Ontario	Mandatory	Protected	Privileged Not admissible in evidence except to prove compliance with reporting obligations
Prince Edward Island	Mandatory	Protected	Privileged Not admissible in evidence except to prove compliance with reporting obligations
Quebec	Discretionary	Protected	Not admissible in evidence except in cases of judicial review of certain decisions of the motor vehicle licensing authority
Saskatchewan	Mandatory	Protected as long as physician acts in good faith	Privileged Not admissible in evidence except to show that the report was made in good faith in accordance with reporting obligation
Yukon	Mandatory	Protected	Not addressed

Section 4
Driving cessation

Alert box

Despite research that shows that life expectancy exceeds driving expectancy by 9.4 years for women and 6.2 years for men,* most current drivers do not plan well for driving cessation.

4.1   Overview

Driving plays a central role in the daily lives of many people, not only as a means of meeting transportation needs, but also as a symbol of autonomy and competence. The prerogative to drive often is synonymous with self-respect, social membership and independence.

Driving cessation can result from a gradual change in driving behavior (i.e., restrictions leading to driving cessation) or as the result of a sudden disabling event (e.g., a stroke) or due to a progressive illness (e.g., dementia). However, decisions to stop driving often are complex and are affected by a number of factors. Sometimes drivers voluntarily stop driving; other times driving cessation is involuntary.

4.2   Voluntary driving cessation

Voluntary driving cessation refers to self-induced changes in driving practices that are made for reasons other than the revocation of a licence or other strong influence from external sources.

A number of general factors are associated with voluntary driving cessation.

- Age — older people are more likely to stop driving of their own accord.
- Gender — women are more likely to give up driving voluntarily.
- Marital status — those who are single, widowed or divorced are more likely to stop driving than those who are married.
- Socioeconomic status — those in lower income brackets are more likely to stop driving.
- Education — people with lower levels of education are more likely to stop driving.

*Foley DJ, Heimovitz HK, Guralnik JM, Brock DB. Driving life expectancy of persons aged 70 years and older in the United States. *Am J Public Health* 2002;92(8):1284-9.

- Place of residence — urban dwellers are more likely to stop driving than those living in rural areas.

These general factors can assist physicians in anticipating who might be more comfortable giving up driving privileges when it becomes medically advisable to stop driving.

Some jurisdictions have initiated programs that use continued driving privileges as a means to motivate people to remain active and maintain their health. One such "wellness" program in the Beauce region of Quebec has shown that older drivers will make efforts to maintain their driving permits when the possibility of prolonging their driving privileges through a healthy lifestyle is explained to them. Similar programs that do not use the maintenance of driving privileges as an incentive were much less successful in influencing healthy lifestyle and habits.

4.3   Involuntary driving cessation

Involuntary driving cessation occurs when a licence is revoked or outside sources (physician, family members) bring their influence to bear. Involuntary driving cessation often is due to the presence of one or more medical conditions or the medications used to treat those conditions.

The most difficult situation physicians face is when a patient is functionally incapable of driving safely, but perceives him- or herself as competent to drive. Physician interventions include frank but sensitive discussions with the patient (with or without the patient's family), referral for a driving evaluation and reporting to the licensing authority. Counseling on alternative means of mobility is needed. For those with cognitive impairment, "through the door" service as opposed to regular "door to door" public transportation will be needed. For progressive illnesses (e.g., dementia), early discussions can help the person and family plan for the inevitable need to stop driving.

Involuntary driving cessation is more likely to be required when awareness of ability declines or is impaired (e.g., dementia). Factors associated with involuntary driving cessation include

- Gender — men are more likely to require outside intervention to cease driving.
- Insight — those with impaired insight are more likely to continue to drive and require intervention.

These factors can assist physicians in predicting who may be resistant to discussions about the need for driving cessation or who will be resistant to and non-compliant with advice or a directive to stop driving. In addition to patients, families also may lack insight into the impact of an illness on driving. Family members may have other reasons for having the person continue to drive (loss of mobility for both patient and caregivers, fear of increased caregiver burden, etc.). Education and support for caregivers and other family members frequently are necessary.

Specialized support groups may be available to assist patients and caregivers make the transition between being a driver and becoming a "non-driver."

4.4   Strategies for discussing driving cessation*

It is important to recognize the consequences of driving cessation for both patients and families. The following suggestions will help physicians develop a strategy before meeting with the patient to discuss driving cessation.

- Before the appointment, consider the patient's impairments. It may be important to ask if the spouse or other caregiver can be present. This can provide emotional support and help to ensure that the family understands that the person needs to stop driving.
- Whenever possible, the appointment should be in a private setting where everyone can be seated. Always address the patient preferentially, both in the initial greeting and in the discussion.
- For patients with progressive illnesses, such as dementia, discuss driving early in the course of the condition, before it becomes a problem. Early discussions also allow patients and family members to prepare for the day when driving is no longer an option.
- Be aware that patient and caregiver reports of driving competence often do not reflect actual competence. Evidence of impaired driving performance from an external source (e.g., driving assessment, record of motor vehicle crashes or "near misses") can be helpful. Include a discussion of the risks of continuing to drive with the patient and family members.
- Focus on the need to stop driving, using the driving assessment, if available, as the appropriate focus.
- Often the patient will talk about his or her past good driving record. Acknowledge that accomplishment in a genuine manner, but return to the need to stop driving. Sometimes saying "medical conditions can make even the best drivers unsafe" also can help to refocus the discussion.
- It is common for drivers, especially those who are older, to talk about a wide range of accomplishments that are intended, somehow, to show there could not be a problem now. Again, acknowledge those accomplishments, but follow with "Things change. Let's not talk about the past. We need to focus on the present" to end that line of conversation and refocus the discussion.
- Ask how the person is feeling and acknowledge his or her emotions. Avoid lengthy attempts to convince the person through rational explanations. Rational arguments are likely to evoke rebuttals.
- It is likely that emotions and feelings of diminished self-worth are a real issue behind resistance

---

*Adapted from The Pallium Project. (2006). *Clinical engagement of medically at-risk driving*. Edmonton, AB: Author.

to accept advice or direction to stop driving. Explore these feelings with empathy. A focus on the feelings can deflect arguments about the evaluation and the stop-driving directive.

- Ask the patient what he or she understands from the discussion. It may be important to schedule a second appointment to discuss the patient's response further and explore next steps.
- Document all discussions about driving in the patient's chart.

4.5   Compliance

An important consideration with involuntary driving cessation is the issue of compliance. Research indicates that as many as 28% of people with dementia continue to drive despite failing an on-road assessment. Family members play a pivotal role in monitoring and managing compliance with a stop-driving directive. Numerous suggestions have been made to assist family members in getting a patient to stop driving, including hiding the keys, disabling the car, canceling the insurance or selling the car. However, the evidence of the success of these interventions is largely anecdotal.

Section 5
Alcohol

5.1 Overview

Alcohol is a depressant drug that has both sedative and disinhibitory effects. It also impairs a driver's judgement, reflex control and behaviour toward other drivers. Impairment from alcohol use is the highest single risk factor for motor-vehicle-related crashes and injury.

Traditionally, diagnoses of alcohol abuse and alcohol dependence, using *Diagnostic and Statistical Manual of Mental Disorders*, fourth edition (DSM-IV) criteria, have been used to identify drivers who may require intervention (see section 5.2.2, Screening tools). However, these diagnostic criteria alone may not correlate with behaviour suggestive of functional impairment when driving.

People charged by police for impaired driving will have their driving privileges restricted according to provincial legislation. The guidelines provided here are not meant to conflict with such legislation.

In people with alcohol dependence or habituation, withdrawal from alcohol may trigger seizures. For seizures induced by alcohol withdrawal, see section 10.4.7.

5.2 Assessment

5.2.1 Clinical history

Researchers have identified a group of drivers (often referred to as "hard-core drinking drivers") who drive with blood alcohol levels averaging twice the legal limit, have previous driving convictions and licence suspensions, may drive without a valid driving licence and likely need treatment for alcohol dependence.

A number of clinical "red flags" have been identified, which may indicate ongoing alcohol use that will impair ability to drive safely. These indicators include

- driver with at least one previous driving offense, especially an alcohol- or drug-related offence
- driver arrested with blood alcohol concentration of 32.6 mmol/L (equivalent to 0.15% or 150 mg/100 mL) or more (the low risk of detection implies that they have probably driven in this condition previously)
- clinical diagnosis of alcohol dependence or abuse
- resistance to changing drinking-and-driving behaviour, often associated with antisocial tendencies such as aggression and hostility
- concomitant use of illicit drugs (e.g., alcohol and marijuana or alcohol and cocaine* in combination)
- male
- age 25–45 years
- education level: high school or less
- history of prior traffic, or other criminal offences
- risk-taking behaviour in situations other than driving
- evidence of poor judgement in situations other than driving
- evidence of aggression in situations other than driving
- lifestyle associated with fatigue and lack of sleep
- patient intoxicated at time of routine office visit.

People demonstrating drinking and driving behaviour, those showing evidence of driving while impaired and those assessed as having a high probability of driving while impaired should not drive any motor vehicle until further assessed.

Assessment may require referral to the motor vehicle licensing authority, to a physician with expertise in addiction medicine or both. Physicians should be aware that reporting drinking and driving behaviour to licensing authorities in some jurisdictions may lead to suspension of a person's licence pending further assessment. Both alcohol abuse and alcohol dependence (see DSM-IV criteria, Appendix G) require diagnosis and treatment, as both conditions represent a driving risk. Treatment may include referral to a rehabilitation program, attendance at mutual help meetings (e.g., Alcoholics Anonymous) or both.

It is important for primary care physicians to monitor patient compliance with treatment recommendations and recovery, as risk of relapse remains for the duration of the person's life.

---

*Cocaethylene is a dangerous, longer-lasting toxic metabolite formed by the concomitant ingestion of alcohol and cocaine.

Clinical judgement is required in assessing the risk of drinking and driving. Rehabilitation programs may enlist primary care physicians to monitor the success and compliance of patients with the interventions used.

Evidence supports a role for ignition interlock devices for those with repeat drinking and driving offenses, especially those with high recidivism scores on the Research Institute on Addictions Self-Inventory (RIASI), a screening test used by addiction specialists. Not only does ignition interlock technology contribute to improved safety on the road, but it also uses a system of monitoring stations to detect early relapse and provide direction back to treatment resources.

5.2.2 Screening tools

Tools to screen for alcohol dependence and abuse include the CAGE questionnaire (Appendix B) and AUDIT, a 10-question alcohol use disorder identification test (Appendix C). AUDIT detects both excessive drinking and the symptoms of abuse and dependence.

The DSM-IV lists the criteria for diagnosis of substance abuse and substance dependence (Appendix G). The major medical criteria for the diagnosis of alcohol dependence are loss of control and compulsive behaviour related to alcohol ingestion and continued use despite the presence of clinical consequences of alcohol abuse.

Section 6
Drugs

6.1   Overview

Patients taking drugs known to have pharmacologic effects or side effects that can impair the ability to drive should be advised not to drive until their individual response is known or the side effects no longer result in impairment (e.g., patients stabilized on chronic opioid therapy for chronic pain or opioid dependence). Keep in mind that drugs can have unexpected adverse effects as well, which may affect ability to drive.

Concomitant use of several drugs may intensify side effects (e.g., alcohol combined with antihistamines or benzodiazepines). Appropriate assessment is essential, including consideration of substance dependence, to ensure that the risk of the patient being impaired while driving is not compounded. Diagnosis of drug abuse and drug dependence, using the DSM-IV criteria (see Appendix G) has been used to identify drivers who may require intervention.

Patients diagnosed with substance dependence need specialized treatment.

Patients experiencing a withdrawal reaction from psychoactive or psychotropic medications may be temporarily impaired in their driving ability and should be advised to refrain from driving until the acute symptoms have abated.

6.2   Clinical history

In assessing a patient's fitness to drive, the patient's use of all drugs — alone or in combination — should be considered, including alcohol (see "red flags" in section 5.2.1) and prescription, over-the-counter and illicit drugs.

Risk factors that may enhance the risk of driving when impaired by a drug are

- the "red flags" listed in section 5.2.1
- younger or relatively inexperienced drivers, especially males
- elderly drivers who are prescribed benzodiazepines, especially if there is concomitant use of alcohol
- low psychologic constraint
- demonstrated antisocial behaviour
- other demonstrated risk-taking behaviour while driving (e.g., speeding, non-use of seat belts).

6.3   Common drugs

It is important to consider drugs that have a psychoactive effect on the brain or have side effects, either alone or in combination, that affect the central or peripheral nervous system.

6.3.1   Sedatives and hypnotics

Patients taking mild sedatives or short-acting hypnotics (sleeping pills), who experience no drowsiness (other than predictable sleep enhancement), can usually drive any type of motor vehicle without difficulty. However, use of benzodiazepines is a risk for driving in the elderly. Patients who are more heavily sedated for therapeutic reasons should not drive. Concomitant use of alcohol in these situations raises the risk of impairment.

6.3.2   Non-prescription antihistamines, motion-sickness medications and muscle relaxants

Drowsiness and dizziness are frequent — and unpredictable — side effects of older antihistamines, motion-sickness medications and muscle relaxants. The newer "non-drowsy" antihistamines are considered safer, but may have a depressant effect on the central nervous system. Patients using these drugs for the first time must be warned not to drive until it is determined whether they are prone to these side effects.

6.3.3   Opioids

Euphoria, depression or inability to concentrate can follow the use of opiates, such as codeine (prescription or over-the-counter), heroin, morphine and synthetic opioids (e.g., meperidine, fentanyl). Patients should be assessed for side effects, as well as frequency of use, tolerance and dependence. Patients on long-term prescribed opioid analgesic therapy should be monitored for side effects, especially drowsiness.

Patients on a formal opioid agonist maintenance program of methadone or buprenorphine prescribed by a physician are usually eligible for Class 5 and 6 drivers' licences. A waiting period following initiation of an agonist maintenance program is recommended before resuming driving, and clinical monitoring for concomitant use of other drugs is recommended (e.g., urine drug screens). Patients in opioid agonist treatment programs may also be eligible for certain commercial licences. Assessment and follow-up monitoring is tailored to the individual.

6.3.4 Central nervous system stimulants

The side effects of central nervous system stimulants, such as amphetamines and cocaine, are unpredictable and often impair ability to drive safely. Abuse of these drugs is a contraindication to driving.

Prescription use of amphetamines, such as those used for attention deficit and sleep disorders, may not impair ability to drive. These patients should be followed regularly by the prescribing physician.

6.3.5 Hallucinogens

Drugs such as cannabis (marijuana or hashish) and its derivatives, lysergic acid diethylamide (LSD) and methylene dioxy-methamphetamine (MDA) alter perception. Driving is contraindicated if these drugs are causing impairment. Patients using medicinal marijuana must be assessed on an individual basis.

6.3.6 Inhalants

Inhalants, such as solvents, glue, gasoline, etc., are toxic to the central nervous system. Use of these inhalants may also result in substance dependence and impairment of the ability to operate a motor vehicle during acute intoxication or due to chronic damage to the brain.

6.3.7 Antidepressants and antipsychotics

Patients taking antidepressants or antipsychotics should be carefully observed during the initial phase of dose adjustment and advised not to drive if they show any evidence of drowsiness or hypotension. Patients who are stable on maintenance doses can usually drive any class of motor vehicle if they are symptom free.

6.3.8   Anticonvulsants

Some of the drugs used to control epileptic seizures can cause drowsiness in some patients, particularly when first prescribed or when dose is increased. Patients should be closely observed and warned not to drive while this side effect persists. Patients taking these drugs may also be restricted from driving due to the underlying seizure disorder. Patients should be advised of the risk of seizure activity and the potential for driving restriction that may occur with dose adjustments.

6.3.9   Conscious sedation in an outpatient setting

Patients should be advised not to drive for 24 hours following conscious sedation (see section 21, Anesthesia and surgery).

6.3.10   Anti-infective agents

Heavy doses of some anti-infective agents or therapeutic doses in some instances may cause drowsiness or imbalance. Patients should be warned not to drive if these side effects occur.

6.3.11   Anticholinergics

These drugs frequently cause sedation and delirium (acute onset of cognitive deficits often associated with hallucinations and fluctuating levels of consciousness), especially in older people. Patients (and their families) should be warned that people who develop these side effects should not drive.

Section 7
Aging

7.1   Overview

Most, if not all, of the health-related conditions listed in this guide that affect driving are more prevalent in the older age groups. Of all age groups, those over 65 years of age have the highest crash rate per kilometre driven.

However, high crash rates in older people cannot be explained by age-related changes alone. In fact, by avoiding unnecessary risk and having the most experience, healthy senior drivers are among the safest drivers on the road. Rather, it is the presence and accumulation of health-related impairments that affect driving that is the major cause of crashes in older people. Because older age per se does not lead to higher crash rates, age-based restrictions on driving are inappropriate.

7.2   Assessment

Age-related changes in vision, reaction time and coordination may have an impact on driving ability. Aging can also affect sensory input (vision, position sense), motor output (reaction time, power, coordination) and the speed of cognitive processing, as well as attention and the scanning abilities that are essential for safe driving. Compensatory driving strategies at the strategic (planning when and where to drive) and tactical (using defensive driving strategies) levels can sometimes compensate for physical impairments that decrease driving capabilities. For example, by driving only in optimum weather and traffic conditions and increasing following distance, deficits in reaction time or braking response may be accommodated.

When a patient's ability to drive safely is not clear, further evaluation may be necessary. Specialized driving assessment centres (see Appendix E) provide on-road driving assessment by trained professionals. The cost is the responsibility of the patient. In 2004, the American

Medical Association released a consensus-based physicians' guide to the assessment and counseling of older drivers; however, the scientific validity of the approach awaits confirmation.

7.3 Specific assessment

Factors that should be considered in the assessment of older drivers spell out the mnemonic SAFEDRIVE.*

Safety record	Is there a history of driving problems?
Attentional skills	Does patient experience lapses of consciousness or episodes of disorientation?
Family report	What are family's observations of driving ability?
Ethanol	Screen for alcohol abuse
Drugs	Review medication, especially for psychoactive drugs
Reaction time	Are neurologic and musculoskeletal disorders slowing reactions?
Intellectual impairment	Complete Mini-mental State Examination
Vision	Test for visual acuity
Executive function	Does the patient have trouble planning and sequencing tasks and self-monitoring behaviour?

7.3.1 Cognitive impairment

Cognitive impairment in older people is almost always due to depression, delirium or dementia. Therefore, treatment of depressive symptoms and the search for remediable causes of delirium (including psychoactive medications, metabolic disturbances, hypoxia and infection) should be considered. See section 7.3.3.

7.3.2 Multiple physical deficits

The accumulation of multiple physical deficits that individually may not affect driving may have an additive effect. If physicians are in doubt about the driving ability of a patient, refer him or her for testing at a specialized on- and off-road driving centre (if available) that is approved by the provincial or territorial ministry of transportation (see Appendix E).

7.3.3 Dementia

The prevalence of dementia, the most common form of cognitive impairment, is approximately 8% for people over 65 years of age, increasing to 30% for those over 90 years.

---

*Wiseman EJ, Souder E. The older driver: a handy tool to assess competence behind the wheel. *Geriatrics* 1996;51:36-45.

However, the diagnosis of dementia alone is not sufficient to remove a person's driver's licence.

The conclusions of multiple consensus groups on this issue are quite similar:

- Clinicians should counsel people with progressive dementia (and their families) that giving up driving is an inevitable consequence of their disease. Strategies to ease this transition should occur early in the clinical course of the disease.
- Moderate to severe dementia is a contraindication to driving. Moderate dementia is defined as the inability to independently perform two or more instrumental activities of daily living (including medication management, banking, shopping, telephone use, cooking) or any basic activity of daily living (eating, dressing, bathing, toileting, transferring).
- The driving ability of people with mild dementia should be tested on an individual basis. Studies have shown that a significant percentage of those in the early stages of dementia are able to operate a motor vehicle safely.

The recommended method for testing driving ability of people with mild dementia is a comprehensive off- and on-road test at a specialized driving centre approved by the provincial or territorial ministry of transportation. People with mild dementia who are deemed fit to continue driving should be re-evaluated, and possibly retested, every 6–12 months.

No test, including the Mini-mental State Examination (MMSE) has sufficient sensitivity or specificity to be used as a single determinant of driving ability. However, abnormalities on tests including the MMSE, clock drawing and Trails B should trigger further in-depth testing of driving ability.

See Appendix D: Driving and dementia toolkit.

7.4   Drugs
See section 6, Drugs.

7.5   Driving cessation
See section 4, Driving cessation.

Section 8
Sleep disorders

Alert box

If a physician believes that a patient is likely to be at risk for driving because of a symptomatic sleep disorder and the patient refuses investigation by a sleep study or refuses appropriate treatment, that patient should not drive any class of motor vehicle.

8.1   Overview

Somnolence (sleepiness), with its associated reduction in vigilance, is an important contributor to driver error and motor vehicle crashes. Somnolence can be due to lifestyle issues, a sleep disorder or both.

There are 8 categories of sleep disorders as outlined in the second edition of the *International Classification of Sleep Disorders*.* These are: insomnias, sleep-related breathing disorders, hypersomnias of central origin, circadian rhythm sleep disorders, parasomnias, sleep-related movement disorders, unclassified disorders, and other sleep disorders.

The recommendations that follow relate primarily to obstructive sleep apnea and narcolepsy, the two sleep disorders for which there is a reasonably clear association between the disorder and the risk of a motor vehicle crash.

8.2   Assessment

Patients reporting excessive somnolence should be carefully questioned about the adequacy and regularity of their sleep–wake cycle, as attention to this may improve symptoms and reduce driving risk.

Risk factors for sleep-related crashes include
- holding multiple jobs
- working night shift
- nighttime driving (between midnight and 6 am)

---

*International classification of sleep disorders, revised: diagnostic and coding manual, 2nd edition, 2005. American Academy of Sleep Medicine. Available: www.absm.org/PDF/ICSD.pdf

---

- less than 6 hours of nighttime sleep
- long duration driving or driving after being awake more than 15 hours
- past history of drowsy driving
- daytime sleepiness
- recent (within a year) at-fault motor vehicle crash.

Patients with various sleep disorders may also have one or more of these risk factors and, as a result, have varying levels of sleepiness. This may partly explain observed differences in risk of operating a motor vehicle. The appropriateness of and need for medical intervention in the management of these disorders also varies.

Patients with excessive daytime somnolence should be questioned about the following risk factors for sleep apnea:

- chronic heavy snoring
- nocturnal snorting and gasping
- witnessed apnea
- uncontrolled hypertension
- significant cardiovascular disease
- morning headaches
- craniofacial abnormalities (e.g., macroglossia, retrognathia)
- large neck size (≥ 43 cm [17 inches])
- obesity.

Males and patients over age 40 are also at increased risk of sleep apnea.

Patients with excessive somnolence and one or more risk factors for sleep apnea, or those with persistent sleepiness and a history consistent with another sleep disorder (e.g., narcolepsy), should be considered for assessment in a sleep laboratory, where such resources are available.

8.3 Obstructive sleep apnea

Obstructive sleep apnea (OSA) is characterized by repetitive upper airway obstruction during sleep, leading to recurring episodes of hypoxemia and arousal from sleep, resulting in disturbed sleep patterns. The relative risk for motor vehicle crashes for patients with symptomatic OSA is about 2 to 3 times that of control groups. In severe cases of OSA, the risk of a motor vehicle crash may be increased as much as 10-fold. However, determining individual risk remains difficult due to individual variations in susceptibility to sleepiness, use of countermeasures or driving avoidance.

Treatment of OSA with continuous positive airway pressure (CPAP) or uvulopalatopharyngoplasty (UPPP) has been successful in reducing crash risk to control levels. Reassessment of patients using CPAP, with a compliance-metering device on the CPAP unit, should be done 1–2 months after diagnosis. The effectiveness of UPPP is less clear and patients treated by this method may require re-evaluation by sleep study.

Some patients with mild cases of sleep apnea may be treated through behavioural modification (e.g., weight reduction, modifying sleeping position, eliminating alcohol and sedatives before sleep or through the use of oral appliances). These interventions may be sufficient, but patients require reassessment for efficacy of treatment before resumption of driving.

Driving recommendations for patients with OSA

The following recommendations should only be made by physicians familiar with the interpretation of sleep studies.

- Regardless of apnea severity, all patients with OSA are subject to sleep schedule irregularities and subsequent sleepiness. Because impairment from sleep apnea, sleep restriction and irregular sleep schedules may be interactive, all patients should be advised about the dangers of driving when drowsy.
- Patients with mild OSA without daytime somnolence who report no difficulty with driving are at low risk for motor vehicle crashes and should be safe to drive any type of motor vehicle.
- Patients with OSA, documented by a sleep study, who are compliant with CPAP or who have had successful UPPP treatment, should be safe to drive any type of motor vehicle.
- Patients with moderate to severe OSA, documented by sleep study, who are *not* compliant with treatment and are considered at increased risk for motor vehicle crashes by the treating physician, should not drive any type of motor vehicle.
- Patients with a high apnea-hypopnea index, especially if associated with right heart failure or excessive daytime somnolence, should be considered at high risk for motor vehicle crashes.
- Patients with OSA who are believed to be compliant with treatment but who are subsequently involved in a motor vehicle crash in which they were at fault should not drive for at least 1 month. During this period, their compliance with therapy must be reassessed. After the 1-month period, they may or may not drive depending on the results of the reassessment.

8.4   Narcolepsy

Narcolepsy is characterized by recurrent lapses into sleep that are often sudden, irresistible and typically last 10–15 minutes. Narcolepsy may be accompanied by cataplexy (sudden bilateral loss of muscle tone) during wakefulness, sleep paralysis (generalized inability to move or to speak during the sleep–wake transition) and vivid hallucinations at sleep onset.

Although there is a clear association between crash risk and narcolepsy, this association is not as well studied as that between crash risk and OSA.

Up to 40% of people with narcolepsy may report sleep-related motor vehicle crashes. Their risk for crashes is about 4 times that of control groups. Patients with cataplexy and sleep paralysis are believed to be at greatest risk for crashes, based on the relative unpredictability of these symptoms. In one study of narcoleptic patients with cataplexy, 42% reported having experienced cataplexy while driving and 18% reported sleep paralysis while driving. There is little information on the effect of treatment on risk for crashes.

Driving recommendations for narcoleptic patients
- Patients with a diagnosis of narcolepsy supported by a sleep study and with uncontrolled episodes of cataplexy during the past 12 months (with or without treatment) should not drive any type of motor vehicle.
- Patients with a diagnosis of narcolepsy supported by a sleep study and with uncontrolled daytime sleep attacks or sleep paralysis in the past 12 months (with or without treatment) should not drive any type of motor vehicle.
- Generally, patients with narcolepsy should not drive commercial vehicles, as long distance driving can be difficult for these patients to manage without significant hypersomnolence. However, people with narcolepsy who are able to maintain a regular sleep–wake cycle may be able to drive commercial vehicles during the day, over short routes.

8.5   Other sleep disorders

Although short- and long-term insomnia may be the most common category of sleep disorder, there are no data linking increased motor vehicle crashes with insomnia.

Circadian rhythm sleep disorders, which are related to sleep loss from disruption of the daily sleep cycle as seen with shift work or "jet lag" experienced with transmeridian flights, are common and might easily be associated with a large number of crashes.

However, there are again no clear data linking them with crashes.

Accordingly, physicians can only make general recommendations about the hazards of drowsy driving due to sleep disorders.

Section 9
Psychiatric illness

Alert box

Immediate contraindications to driving*:

- acute psychosis
- condition relapses sufficient to impair perceptions, mood or thinking
- medication with potentially sedating effects initiated or dose increased
- lack of insight or lack of cooperation with treatment
- lack of compliance with any conditional licensing limitations imposed by motor vehicle licensing authority
- suicidal plan involving crashing a vehicle
- an intent to use vehicle to harm others.

*A patient seen or reported to have any of these problems should be advised not to drive until the condition is evaluated and treated.

9.1   Overview

Determining fitness to drive in a patient with a psychiatric illness is often complex. There is a great deal of individual variation in patients with psychiatric illness, particularly in the critical area of insight, and multiple conditions often coexist. Many psychiatric disorders are chronic and subject to relapse, and require ongoing monitoring.

The adverse effects of treatment or medication may pose a hazard to driving ability (see Section 6, Drugs). However, these individuals may well be safer drivers with psychotropic drugs than without them.

The term "psychiatric illness" encompasses numerous cognitive, emotional and behavioural disorders. The DSM-IV uses a multi-axial diagnostic description:

Axis I	clinical psychiatric disorder(s), including substance-use disorders
Axis II	personality disorder(s) — 10 types are defined
Axis III	concurrent general medical illnesses and injuries

cont'd

Axis IV	psychosocial stressors (life events and problems)
Axis V	global assessment of functioning (GAF): a score of 100 = maximum level of functioning

Although driving risk researchers have focused on Axis I and Axis II diagnoses, Axis IV and Axis V issues need to also be considered in assessing fitness to drive in a patient with psychiatric illness. Factors such as sleep deprivation, fatigue, stress or a predisposition to anxiety may aggravate existing problems. A score of less than 50 on GAF should alert the physician that further assessment is needed.

9.2 Functional impairment

Good cognitive ability is the foundation of competent driving. Cognitive ability refers to how we select, interpret, remember and use information to make judgements and decisions. **Psychiatric illnesses may affect thinking, mood and/or perception, resulting in a wide range of types and degrees of cognitive impairment.**

Neuropsychologic testing is the "gold standard" for assessing cognitive ability, but it is time consuming, and the required resources are limited and generally located in urban areas. This testing is only predictive of driving when significant cognitive impairment is present (unsafe to drive) or no cognitive impairment is present (likely safe to drive). In situations where minimal or mild impairment is found, further evaluation may be required. For simple cases, in-office cognitive screening is useful. Complex cases, or those that involve commercial drivers, may require the additional expertise and resources of a driver assessment centre.

Insight is critical for drivers to drive within their limitations and to know how and when these limitations change. Poor insight in patients with psychiatric illness may be evidenced by noncompliance with treatment, trivializing their role in a crash or repeated involuntary admissions to hospital (often as a result of discontinuing prescribed medication).

A driver's ability to be aware of any cognitive limitations should be assessed, as well as judgement and willingness to adapt his or her driving to these limitations.

9.3 Assessing fitness to drive

In general, drivers with a psychiatric illness are fit to drive if
- the psychiatric condition is stable (not in the acute phase)
- functional cognitive impairment is assessed as minimal (adequate alertness, memory, attention and executive function abilities)
- the patient is compliant and consistent with prescribed psychotropic medication
- the maintenance dose of medication does not cause noticeable sedation
- the patient has the insight to self-limit at times of symptom relapse and to seek assessment promptly

- the patient's family is supportive of his or her driving.

Consider further assessment if

- a family member reports a concern
- an at-fault accident occurs
- there is uncertainty about the degree of cognitive impairment.

9.4   Specific illnesses

9.4.1   Schizophrenia

Schizophrenia is associated with cognitive impairment, slowed reaction times and a variable degree of distraction that may depend on the perceptual distortions present at any time. Early identification of this illness and the use of newer antipsychotic agents can do much to preserve social and cognitive functioning.

9.4.2   Personality disorders

Personality disorders (Axis II of DSM-IV) are a more controversial area. The locus of distress is often with others, not with the individual given the diagnosis. By definition, the behavioural pattern is considered to be persistent and the diagnosis often has a pejorative or dismissive tone.

"Cluster B" personality disorders (including antisocial personality disorder, borderline personality disorder, histrionic personality disorder and narcissistic personality disorder) may be associated with behaviour such as aggression, egocentricity, impulsiveness, resentment of authority, intolerance of frustration and irresponsibility.

9.4.3   Depression and bipolar disorder

Depression impairs cognitive function, sometimes sufficiently to present as "pseudo-dementia." Some individuals with mood disorders, even when treated to full remission, have residual non-progressive cognitive dysfunction in short-term memory, concentration or mental processing speed.

A manic episode is a contraindication to driving; fitness to return to driving will depend on response to treatment and the patient's level of insight and degree of inter-episode functioning. If a patient with bipolar disorder is advised not to drive, consent should be sought to notify a family member, and these communications should be documented. Non compliance with medical advice not to drive should be reported to licensing authorities.

Suicide has also been attributed to the removal of driving privileges, usually in older males. This risk emphasizes the usefulness of social and educational programs that help those facing an unexpected transition when they lose their driving licence for medical reasons.

Most treatment of depression is with newer generation drugs rather than the older tricyclic agents. Tricyclics have been associated with an increased risk of motor vehicle crashes, especially at higher doses, or if multiple agents are used. Selective serotonin reuptake inhibitors (SSRIs) are less likely to cause cognitive impairment.

Electroconvulsive therapy (ECT) can induce sustained confusion in 1 in 200 patients. Those receiving outpatient ECT need to comply with standard guidelines for not driving after anesthesia and take extra time if they are experiencing any memory problems after ECT.

Rapid-rate transcranial magnetic stimulation (rTMS) is reported to produce no evidence of cognitive impairment

9.4.4   Anxiety disorders

Anxiety disorders may cause motor vehicle crashes when the level of driver anxiety interferes with concentration or causes "freezing" or perseverative errors.

Severe motor vehicle crashes commonly cause subsequent psychiatric disorders. When post-traumatic stress disorder symptoms or phobic avoidance complicate the picture, crash survivors can get significant help in the healing process through counseling and from relevant books.

Benzodiazepines may increase the risk of motor vehicle crashes.

9.4.5   Psychotic episodes

These may be the most urgent psychiatric disorders to deal with. An acute episode is incompatible with safe driving. Physicians should note that an acutely psychotic patient may be able to mask symptoms initially.

Even drivers with Class 4 licences (e.g., taxi) may be safe to return to driving once the acute episode has settled, if there are no impairing effects from maintenance medication and if there is sufficient insight to comply with treatment and identify early indicators of relapse.

9.4.6   Attention deficit hyperactivity disorder (ADHD)

The motor vehicle licensing authority, as well as the parents of children diagnosed with ADHD who qualify for a driver's licence, should pay close attention to speeding, red light infractions and risk-taking behaviour.

As a group, novice drivers with ADHD, when driving without the benefit of stimulant medication, appear to have an elevated risk of crashes compared with their age cohort as a whole. Although ADHD is now seen as a life-long disorder, it is unclear why the prevalence decreases with age and whether this may reflect learned adaptive strategies. For both children and adults, psychostimulant medication may have a useful role in controlling symptoms and improving performance in a number of tasks. Stimulants most likely reduce the risk of moving violations and crashes for drivers with ADHD, particularly in the first 5 years of driving. Although their efficacy in real driving situations remains to be determined, long-acting stimulants, which provide medication coverage throughout both the day and night, will likely reduce driving risk in this population.

9.4.7 Aggressive driving

Law enforcement agencies are paying more attention to ticketing aggressive drivers as the hazards associated with "road rage" become more evident.

No prospective studies of the relation between psychiatric disorders and "road rage" were found, nor any studies that targeted high-risk groups, such as individuals with a diagnosis of intermittent explosive disorder, ADHD, or attendees at therapy groups for perpetrators of domestic violence.

With the present state of knowledge, it seems reasonable to refer aggressive drivers with insight for specialized cognitive behaviour therapy groups. Those without insight will likely only be dealt with by court-ordered treatment.

9.5 Psychoactive drugs

Psychoactive medications may impair ability to drive. See Section 6.3.7

Section 10
Nervous system

10.1   Overview

Safe driving requires concentration, a reasonable level of intelligence and maturity, complete control over all muscle movements and freedom from the distracting influence of severe pain. In addition, a safe driver must always be alert, fully conscious and capable of quickly appreciating and responding to changing traffic and road conditions.

This section lists and discusses the most common neurologic conditions that can adversely affect driving ability.

10.2   Febrile or toxic seizures, benign childhood absence epilepsy and other age-related epilepsy syndromes

Where seizures are directly related to a toxic illness, either in childhood or in adult life, and the patient has fully recovered from the illness, the seizures are of no concern in evaluating a patient's later medical fitness to drive. Some benign childhood epilepsy syndromes remit. These would be of less concern than a current epileptic disorder. A neurologic evaluation should be obtained in all such cases.

10.3   Syncope

A single occurrence of syncope that is fully explained and, based on the etiology, is unlikely to recur may require no more than careful observation. However, patients who have a history of a number of fainting spells or repeated unexplained falls should not drive until the cause has been determined and successful corrective measures taken.

See section 13.4, Syncope.

10.4   Seizures

As for all conditions, in all instances where a temporal recommendation is made, the time period should be considered a general guideline. Individual circumstances may warrant prolonging or reducing the time period suggested.

The recommendations for seizures are presented in both tabular (Table 2) and textual format.

10.4.1   *Single, unprovoked seizure before a diagnosis*

Private drivers: These patients should not drive for *at least 3 months* and not before a complete neurologic evaluation — including electroencephalography (EEG) with waking and sleep recording and appropriate neurologic imaging, prefereably magnetic resonance imaging (MRI) — has been carried out to determine the cause.

Commercial drivers: Commercial drivers should be told to stop driving all classes of vehicles at once. For these drivers, there is a need for even greater certainty that another seizure will not occur while they are driving. As a minimum, commercial drivers should follow the private driver guideline and not drive private vehicles for at least 3 months after a single, unprovoked seizure. If a complete neurologic evaluation, including waking and sleep EEG and appropriate neurologic imaging, preferably MRI, does not suggest a diagnosis of epilepsy or some other condition that precludes driving, it is safe to recommend a return to commercial driving after the patient has been seizure free for 12 months.

Table 2: Recommendations for drivers who have experienced seizures

Type of seizure	Private drivers	Commercial drivers
Single, unprovoked seizure before a diagnosis	• No driving for at least 3 months and • Neurologic assessment, preferably including EEG (awake and asleep) and appropriate imaging	• No driving private vehicles for at least 3 months • Neurologic assessment, including EEG (awake and asleep) and appropriate imaging • If no epilepsy diagnosis, resume professional driving if seizure free for 12 months
After diagnosis of epilepsy	Drive if • 6 months seizure free* on medication • Physician has insight into patient compliance • Physician cautions against fatigue, alcohol	• Resume driving if 5 years seizure free (Recommendations for individual patients may differ on an exceptional basis.)

cont'd

After surgery to prevent epileptic seizures	• Resume driving if 12 months seizure free after surgery with therapeutic drug levels (Recommendations for individual patients may differ on an exceptional basis.)	• Resume driving if 5 years seizure free (Recommendations for individual patients may differ on an exceptional basis.)
Seizures only in asleep or immediately on wakening	• Drive after 1 year from initial seizure if drug levels are therapeutic	• No driving commercial vehicles for at least 5 years
Medication withdrawal or change:		
Initial withdrawal or change	• No driving for 3 months from the time medication is discontinued or changed	• No driving for 6 months from the time medication is discontinued or changed
If seizures recur after withdrawal or change	• Resume driving if seizure free for 3 months	• Resume driving if seizure free for 6 months (Recommendations for individual patients may differ on an exceptional basis.)
Long-term withdrawal and discontinuation of medication	• Drive any vehicle if seizure free off medication for 5 years with no epileptiform activity within previous 6 months on waking and sleep EEG	
Auras (simple partial seizures)	Drive if: • Seizures are unchanged for at least 12 months • No generalized seizures • Neurologist approves • No impairment in level of consciousness or cognition • No head or eye deviation with seizures	Drive if: • Seizures remain benign for at least 3 years • No generalized seizures • Neurologist approves • No impairment in level of consciousness or cognition • No head or eye deviation with seizures
Alcohol-withdrawal-induced seizures	Drive if: • Remain alcohol free and seizure free for 6 months • Complete a recognized rehabilitation program for substance dependence • Compliant with treatment	
Post-traumatic seizures (single, not epilepsy)	• Same as for single, unprovoked seizure	
Juvenile myoclonic epilepsy (Janz syndrome)	• No driving of any class of vehicle unless taking appropriate anti-seizure medication	

*Or 12 months seizure free if seizures associated with altered awareness have occurred in previous 2 years (see text).
Note: EEG = electroencelphalography; MRI = magnetic resonance imaging

10.4.2   After a diagnosis of epilepsy

Patients may drive any class of vehicle if they have been seizure free for 5 years with or without anticonvulsive medication. However, patients with Juvenile myoclonic epilepsy (Janz syndrome) may not drive any class of vehicle unless they are taking appropriate anti-seizure medication.

Private drivers: Patients with epilepsy who are taking anti-seizure medication should not be recommended for Class 5 or 6 licensing until the following conditions are met:

- *Seizure-free period:* The patient should be seizure free on medication for not less than 6 months, unless seizures with altered awareness have occurred more than once a year in the previous 2 years, in which case the seizure-free interval should be 12 months. With certain types of epilepsy, this period may be reduced to not less than 3 months on the recommendation of a neurologist, stating the reasons for this recommendation. The seizure-free period is necessary to establish a drug level that prevents further seizures without side effects that could affect the patient's ability to drive safely. The anti-seizure medication should have no evident effect on alertness or muscular coordination.

- *Patient compliance with medication and instructions:* The attending physician should feel confident that the patient is conscientious and reliable and will continue to take the prescribed anti-seizure medication as directed, carefully follow the physician's instructions and promptly report any further seizures. Medication compliance and dose appropriateness should be documented with drug levels whenever reasonably possible.

Physicians should advise epileptic patients that they should not drive for long hours without rest or when fatigued. Patients who require anti-seizure medication and who are known to drink alcohol to excess should not drive until they have been alcohol and seizure free for at least 6 months. These patients often neglect to take their medication while drinking. As well, alcohol withdrawal is known to precipitate seizures and the use of even moderate amounts of alcohol may lead to greater impairment in the presence of anti-seizure medication. Patients taking these drugs should be advised not to consume more than 1 unit of alcohol per 24 hours.

A patient who stops taking anti-seizure medication against medical advice should not be recommended for driving. This prohibition on driving may change if the physician feels confident that the formerly noncompliant patient, who is again taking anti-seizure medication as prescribed, will conscientiously do so in the future and if compliance is corroborated by therapeutic drug levels, when available.

Commercial drivers: It can be unsafe for commercial drivers who must take anti-seizure medication to operate passenger-carrying or commercial transport vehicles (Classes 1–4). For these drivers, there is a need for even greater certainty that another seizure will not occur while they are driving. Commercial drivers are often unable to avoid driving for long periods of time, frequently under extremely adverse conditions or in highly stressful and fatiguing situations that could precipitate another seizure. Unfortunately, seizures do sometimes recur even after many years of successful treatment.

10.4.3   *After surgery to prevent epileptic seizures*

Private drivers: These patients should be seizure free for 12 months after the surgery and taking anti-seizure medication before being recommended for driving any type of motor vehicle. This period may be reduced to 6 months on the recommendation of a neurologist.

Commercial drivers: Before resuming driving, commercial drivers should be seizure free for

5 years with or without medication. However, in certain types of epilepsy, this period may be reduced to 3 years on the recommendation of a neurologist.

10.4.4 Seizures only while asleep or on wakening

Private drivers: Patients with epilepsy whose seizures have only occurred while they were asleep or immediately after wakening for at least 1 year can be recommended for a private licence (Classes 5 and 6) no less than 12 months after the initial seizure and with therapeutic drug levels.

Commercial drivers: Commercial drivers with these types of seizures and with therapeutic drug levels should not drive passenger-carrying vehicles or commercial trucks (Classes 1–4) for at least 5 years. Recommendations for individual patients may differ on an exceptional basis. There should be no prolonged postictal impairment in wakefulness.

10.4.5 Withdrawal of seizure medication or medication change

These recommendations do not apply to voluntary cessation of anti-seizure medication by the patient or missed doses of prescribed medication.

Initial withdrawal or change: Some patients with fully controlled seizures whose anti-seizure medication is withdrawn or changed have a recurrence of their seizures. Because the relapse rate with drug withdrawal is at least 30%–40%, patients must not drive for 3 months from the time their medication is discontinued or changed. Such patients should always be cautioned that they could have further seizures and counseled as to risk factors for seizure recurrence.

The same concerns and conditions apply to commercial drivers as to private drivers. However, the period of observation before resuming driving is 6 months, and a normal EEG, preferably in both wakefulness and sleep, should be obtained during this time. If the evaluation is being done in the context of medication withdrawal, the EEG should be done with non-measurable serum drug levels.

If seizures recur: When seizures recur after a physician has ordered a discontinuation of, or a change in, anti-seizure medication, patients can resume driving provided they take the previously effective medication according to the physician's instructions. Private drivers must also have been seizure free for 3 months and commercial drivers for 6 months before resuming driving.

Long-term withdrawal or discontinuation: Patients with epilepsy whose anticonvulsant medication has been discontinued can drive any class of vehicle when they have been seizure free off medication for 5 years and no epileptiform activity is recorded during a waking and sleep EEG obtained in the 6 months prior to driving.

10.4.6 Auras (simple partial seizures)

Private drivers: Patients with auras with somatosensory, special sensory symptoms or non-disabling focal motor seizures in a single limb without head or eye deviation may be eligible for a Class 5 or 6 licence provided there is no impairment in their level of consciousness and cognition, the seizures are unchanged for more than 1 year and they have the approval of a neurologist to resume driving.

Commercial drivers: Patients with auras with somatosensory, special sensory symptoms or nondisabling focal motor seizures in a single limb without head or eye deviation may be eligible to drive commercial vehicles, including passenger-carrying commercial vehicles (Classes 1–4), provided there is no impairment in their level of consciousness, the seizure pattern has remained benign for at least 3 years and has never been generalized and they have the approval of a neurologist to resume driving.

10.4.7 Seizures induced by alcohol withdrawal

As a result of chronic alcohol abuse or after a bout of heavy drinking, alcohol withdrawal can cause seizures in both epileptic and non-epileptic patients. Patients who have had alcohol withdrawal seizures should not drive any type of motor vehicle. They require investigation to exclude an underlying epileptic disorder. Before they can resume driving, these patients must complete a recognized rehabilitation program for substance dependence and remain both alcohol free and seizure free for 6 months. A non-epileptic patient who has had a seizure induced by alcohol withdrawal does not usually require anti-seizure medication.

10.5 Disorders affecting coordination, muscle strength and control

Loss of muscle strength or coordination occurs in a wide variety of disorders, each of which poses a special problem. This includes such conditions as weakness, altered muscle tone, involuntary movements or reduced coordination due to poliomyelitis, Parkinson's disease, multiple sclerosis, cerebral palsy, the muscular dystrophies, myasthenia gravis, tumours of the brain or spinal cord, spina bifida, organic brain damage following a head injury or stroke, Tourette's syndrome, Huntington's chorea and ataxias.

In the early stages of some of these conditions, no driving restrictions may be necessary. However, in serious cases, it will be immediately obvious that the applicant is unable to drive safely. Drivers with Class 5 licences, who have mild loss of muscle strength or control, may have special controls added to their cars. The motor vehicle licensing authorities are aware of the types of controls available and where they can be obtained. After the controls have been installed, the driver must undergo a road test and satisfy an examiner that he or she can drive safely.

If the disorder is not progressive, one medical examination and road test will usually suffice. However, if the condition is progressive or there are multiple medical conditions, the patient must be followed closely and driving discontinued when the disability reaches a point that makes driving unsafe. In such conditions, the physician should recommend a functional evaluation if the patient wishes to resume driving.

If the condition is characterized by or accompanied by cognitive impairment, impairment of memory, judgement or behaviour or it is liable to lead to a loss of consciousness, the patient should be advised to stop driving. Any sign of cognitive impairment should trigger further evaluation of fitness to drive (see section 7.3).

In most instances, these disorders preclude holding a Class 6 licence.

10.6 Severe pain

Severe pain from such causes as a migraine headache, trigeminal neuralgia or lesions of the cervical or lumbar spine can decrease concentration or limit freedom of movement to a degree that can make driving extremely hazardous. This is a particular concern for commercial drivers whose responsibilities or working conditions may prevent them from stopping work even if the pain becomes disabling.

In addition, prescription and over-the-counter painkillers may interfere with a person's ability to drive safely. However, some patients may be rendered capable of driving despite their pain by the use of these medications. Patients who experience frequent, chronic and incapacitating pain should be advised to avoid driving while incapacitated.

The underlying condition causing the pain may affect the person's fitness to drive and a functional evaluation may be indicated.

10.7 Head injury and seizures

Drivers who have had a recent head injury should always be examined with particular care to determine whether there is any evidence of confusion or other symptoms that would make them temporarily unfit to drive. Although a minor head injury usually does not impair driving for more than a few hours, a more serious injury that results in even minimal residual brain damage or concussion should be fully evaluated before driving is resumed.

See also section 14.4, Traumatic and acquired brain injury.

10.7.1 Post-traumatic seizure

A patient with a head injury may resume driving after a single post-traumatic seizure under certain conditions.

Private drivers: A patient with a single post-traumatic seizure should not drive for at least 3 months and not until a complete neurologic evaluation, including EEG with sleep recording and appropriate brain imaging, has been carried out.

Commercial drivers: A patient with a single post-traumatic seizure should not drive for at least 12 months and not until a complete neurological evaluation, including EEG with sleep recording and appropriate brain imaging, has been carried out.

10.7.2   Post-traumatic epilepsy

The guidelines for private and commercial drivers after a diagnosis of epilepsy (section 10.4.2) should be applied to those with post-traumatic epilepsy.

10.8   Intracranial tumours

A patient who wishes to resume private or commercial driving after removal of an intracranial tumour must be evaluated regularly for recovery of neurologic function and the absence of seizure activity.

10.8.1   Benign tumours

If a patient's cognitive function, judgement, coordination, visual fields, sense of balance, motor power and reflexes are all found to be normal after the removal of a benign intracranial tumour, there is usually no reason to recommend any permanent driving restrictions.

If a seizure occurred either before or after the removal of a tumour, the patient should be seizure free for at least 12 months, with or without medication, before resuming driving.

10.8.2   Malignant tumours

No general recommendation can be made about driving after the removal of a malignant or metastatic brain tumour. The opinions of the consulting neurologist and the surgeon who removed the tumour should always be sought and each case evaluated individually. Seizures related to a brain tumour are discussed above. If there is a possibility that the tumour could recur, the physician should always fully explain to the patient the nature of the condition before sending a medical report to the motor vehicle licensing authority.

Section 11
Vision

11.1   Overview

The following recommendations are based in large part on the work of the Canadian Ophthalmological Society's expert working group on driving and vision standards.

When a patient is visually impaired, the physician should inform the patient of the nature and extent of the visual defect and, if required, report the problem to the appropriate authorities.

When minor visual defects are not accompanied by cognitive defects or neglect, most drivers are capable of compensating for partial defects. For example, most people adapt to the loss of an eye in a period of several months. Recent studies indicate that experienced drivers can compensate for a loss of visual acuity if they are in familiar surroundings and they limit their speed. In these circumstances, functional assessments are indicated.

This section presents information about the recommended visual acuity and visual field needed for safe driving (section 11.2). Actual standards for these functions are set by provincial or territorial licensing authorities and may vary among jurisdictions as well as varying from the recommendations in this section, which are based on expert opinion. The section also presents information about other important visual functions that should be taken into consideration in determining fitness to drive (section 11.3) and recommendations for exceptional cases that require individual assessment (section 11.4). It also provides further detail on recommended testing procedures (addendum 1), a list of medical conditions with increased risk for vision problems and a discussion of the use of vision aids in driving (addendum 2).

11.2   Recommended visual functions

11.2.1   Visual acuity (corrected)

A driver's visual acuity must allow him or her time to detect and react to obstacles, pedestrians, other vehicles and signs while moving at the maximum posted speed, both in daylight and in darkness. Greater levels of visual acuity are required for some classes of licence to ensure public safety. Road signs should be designed to be easily legible at a safe distance for all individuals who meet the minimum visual acuity standard. (See addendum 1 for testing procedures.)

Class of licence	Recommended visual acuity
Private (classes 5, 6)	Not less than 20/50 (6/15) with both eyes open and examined together
Commercial (classes 1, 2, 3, 4)	Not less than 20/30 (6/9) with both eyes open and examined together. Worse eye not less than 20/400 (6/120)*

11.2.2   Visual field*

An adequate continuous field of vision is important to safe driving. Any significant scotoma or restriction in the binocular visual field can make driving dangerous. Conditions often associated with visual field loss are described in addendum 2 of this section. If a visual field defect is suspected (based on medical condition, subjective report or confrontation field assessment), the patient should be referred to an ophthalmologist or optometrist for further testing. (See addendum 1 for testing procedures.)

Class of licence	Recommended visual field
Private (classes 5, 6)	120° continuous along the horizontal meridian and 15° continuous above and below fixation with both eyes open and examined together

cont'd

---

*Several jurisdictions require an acuity higher than 20/400 (6/120) in the worse eye. For example, Quebec has a standard of 20/70 (6/21) and Ontario's is 20/100 (6/30).

Commercial (classes 1, 2, 3, 4)	150° continuous along the horizontal meridian and 20° continuous above and below fixation with both eyes open and examined together

11.2.3 Diplopia

Diplopia (double vision) within the central 40° (i.e., 20° to the left, right, above and below fixation) of primary gaze is incompatible with safe driving for all classes of licence. Individuals who have uncorrected diplopia within the central 40° of primary gaze should be referred to an ophthalmologist or optometrist for further assessment. If the diplopia can be completely corrected with a patch or prisms to meet the appropriate standards for visual acuity and visual field, the individual may be eligible to drive. Before resuming driving with a patch, there should be an adjustment period of 3 months or a period sufficient to satisfy the treating ophthalmologist or optometrist that adequate adjustment has occurred.

11.3   Other important visual functions for driving

11.3.1   Colour vision

Individuals should be made aware of any abnormality of colour vision to allow them to compensate for this difference in their vision. Although no standards exist for colour vision, all drivers should be able to discriminate among traffic lights. (See addendum 1 for testing procedures.)

11.3.2   Contrast sensitivity

Individuals with reduced contrast sensitivity may experience difficulty with driving, in spite of having adequate visual acuity. However, it is unclear at this time what level of reduction in contrast sensitivity represents an unacceptable risk for driving. Loss of contrast sensitivity can be associated with increased age, cataract, refractive surgery as well as other ocular disorders. Individuals should be made aware of any significant reduction in contrast sensitivity.

11.3.3   Depth perception

Motor vehicle crashes sometimes occur because of the driver's inability to judge distances accurately. However, judging distance is a skill that can be learned, even by persons with monocular vision. Monocular judgements of depth can be made based on such cues as the relative size or interposition of objects, clearness of details and analysis of shadows and contrast effects. A more refined form of distance judgement, called stereopsis, is based on information coming from both eyes.

A driver who has recently lost sight in an eye or lost the use of stereopsis may require a few months to recover the ability to judge distance accurately.

11.3.4 Dark adaptation and glare recovery

The ability to adapt to decreased illumination and to recover rapidly from exposure to glaring headlights is of great importance for night driving. The partial loss of these functions in elderly people, particularly those with cataracts or macular disease, may at times justify limiting driving to daylight hours.

11.4 Exceptional cases

The loss of some visual functions can be compensated for adequately, particularly in cases of long-standing or congenital impairments. When a driver becomes visually impaired, the capacity to drive safely varies with the driver's compensatory abilities. As a result, there may be individuals with visual deficits who do not meet the vision standards for driving but who are able to drive safely. On the other hand, there may be individuals with milder deficits who do meet the vision standards but who cannot drive safely.

In these exceptional situations, it is recommended that the individual undergo a special assessment of fitness to drive. The decision regarding fitness to drive can only be made by the appropriate licensing authorities. However, examining physicians may take the following information into consideration when making recommendations to a patient or to the licensing authorities: favourable reports from the ophthalmologist or optometrist; good driving record; stability of the condition; the absence of other significant medical contraindications; other references (e.g., professional, employment, etc.); assessment by a specialist at a recognized rehabilitation or occupational therapy centre for driver training.

In some cases it may be reasonable to recommend that an individual to be granted a restricted or conditional licence to ensure safe driving. It may also be appropriate to make such permits exclusive to a single class of vehicles.

Addendum 1: Testing procedures

A1.1 Visual acuity

The distance visual acuity of applicants should be tested using the refractive correction (spectacles or contact lenses) that they will use for driving. The examiner should assess visual acuity under binocular (both eyes open) or monocular conditions if required by the standard. It is recommended that visual acuity be assessed using a Snellen chart or equivalent at the distance appropriate for the chart under bright photopic lighting conditions of 275 to 375 lux (or greater than 80 candelas/m^2). Charts that are designed to be used at 3 meters or greater are recommended.

Visual field: When a confrontational field assessment is carried out to screen for visual field defects the following procedure is recommended as a minimum:

1. The examiner is standing or seated approximately 0.6 m (2 feet) in front of the examinee with eyes at about the same level.
2. The examiner asks the examinee to fixate on the nose of the examiner with both eyes open.
3. The examiner extends his or her arms forward, positioning the hands halfway between the examinee and the examiner. With arms fully extended, the examiner asks the examinee to confirm when a moving finger is detected.
4. The examiner should confirm that the ability to detect the moving finger is continuously present throughout the area specified in the applicable visual field standard. Testing is recommended in an area of at least 180° horizontal and 40° vertical, centred around fixation.

If a defect is detected, the individual should be referred to an ophthalmologist or optometrist for a full assessment.

When a full assessment is required, the binocular visual field should be assessed using a III/4e Goldmann type target or the closest equivalent. The Esterman functional vision test on the Humphrey visual field analyzer or kinetic perimetry on the Goldmann perimeter are recommended. When binocular assessments are not possible, monocular assessments will be considered.

Some automated testing devices used in driver testing centres have a procedure for assessing visual field. However, these tests are often insensitive to many types of visual field defect and none tests greater than 140° in the horizontal median. Thus, they may not be adequate for screening purposes.

Diplopia: Anyone reporting double vision should be referred to an ophthalmologist or optometrist for further assessment.

Contrast sensitivity: Assessment of contrast sensitivity is recommended for those who are referred to an ophthalmologist or optometrist for vision problems related to driving. Contrast sensitivity may be a more valuable indicator of visual performance in driving than Snellen chart visual acuity. Increased use of this test is encouraged as a supplement to visual acuity assessment.

Contrast sensitivity can be measured using a number of procedures that are commercially available. Examples* include: the Pelli-Robson letter contrast sensitivity chart; either the 25% or the 11% Regan low-contrast acuity chart; the Bailey-Lovie low-contrast acuity chart; and the VisTech contrast sensitivity test. The testing procedures and conditions recommended for the specific test used should be followed.

Colour vision: Any test that requires the discrimination of red, green and yellow can be used to assess colour vision for driving.

---

*This list may not be exhaustive and does not constitute an endorsement.

Depth perception: There are no clinical tests available for assessing depth perception other than those used for stereopsis. If stereopsis assessment is required, the Titmus test can be used.

Dark adaptation and glare recovery: Currently there are no standardized tests or procedures that can be recommended for assessing these functions.

Addendum 2: Medical conditions and vision aids for driving

Medical conditions that may require further assessment for vision problems: Some medical conditions have a greater risk of associated vision problems. Examples include*

Corneal scarring	Eye movement disorders
Refractive surgery	Strabismus
Cataract	Stroke
Diabetic eye disease	Brain tumour and surgery
Retinal disease	Head trauma
Optic nerve disorders	Neurologic disorders
Glaucoma	Multiple sclerosis

There are many other conditions that also cause vision problems. If a vision problem is suspected as a result of a medical condition, it is recommended that the individual be referred to an ophthalmologist or optometrist for further assessment of visual function.

Vision aids and driving: Telescopic spectacles (bioptic devices), hemianopia aids and other low-vision aids may enhance visual function. The problems associated with their use while driving can include loss of visual field, magnification causing apparent motion and the illusion of nearness. Although expert opinion does not support their use by low-vision drivers, recent Canadian legal decisions oblige licensing authorities to evaluate their use on an individual basis for drivers whose vision does not meet the established standards.

These aids cannot be used to enable the user to meet the visual standards. Consequently, a driver must demonstrate that the use of the low-vision aid permits him to drive safely despite his failure to meet the established visual standard. A road test is the usual means of functional assessment in these cases. It should be noted that drivers using telescopic lenses look through the lenses only 5%–10 % of the time he or she is driving. Consequently, some jurisdictions assess the driver without the lenses to evaluate their driving under the conditions that will prevail for 90% of their time behind the wheel.

Section 12
Auditory-vestibular disorders

12.1   Overview

There are few data to indicate that hearing impairment affects driving ability. In certain specific circumstances, meeting certain standards of hearing is recommended. Vestibular dysfunction causing vertigo may affect ability to drive.

12.2   Hearing

12.2.1   Standards

There are no hearing standards for private drivers in Canada.

The following standards are recommended as applied to the person's better ear.

If a hearing-impaired person drives a Class 2 or 4 vehicle, he or she should first undergo an audiogram performed by an audiologist or otolaryngologist. Drivers with Class 2 or 4 licences should have a corrected hearing loss of no more than 40 dB averaged at 500, 1000 and 2000 Hz and a corrected word recognition score of at least 50%–60%.

Drivers of Classes 1 and 3 vehicles who wish to drive in the United States must meet the same standards as outlined above for drivers of class 2 and 4. Although no hearing standards apply for holders of Class 1, 3, 5 or 6 licences in Canada, drivers transporting dangerous goods, regardless of the class of vehicle, should meet the standards for Class 2 and 4 licences as noted in the previous paragraph.

12.2.2   Hearing assistive devices

Hearing aids or cochlear implants amplify ambient noise. This may cause fatigue or annoyance. If not functioning properly, they may mask warning sounds that the driver should be able to hear.

12.3   Vestibular disorders

There are three fundamental types of vestibular disorders, all of which can seriously affect driving ability.

12.3.1   Acute unilateral vestibular dysfunction — single prolonged episode

Patients with acute unilateral vestibular disorders, such as labyrinthitis or vestibular neuronitis, should be advised not to drive until their condition has subsided and the acute symptoms have resolved.

12.3.2   Recurrent unilateral vestibular dysfunction

- Patients with Meniere's disease or other recurrent vestibulopathies should be advised to pull off the road at the first sign of an acute attack, until their symptoms subside. Those prone to severe, prolonged attacks may wish to avoid driving long distances alone.
- Patients experiencing acute episodes without warning symptoms, particularly those with Tumarkin's (non-syncopal drop) attacks, should not drive until their symptoms have been controlled or have abated for at least 6 months.
- Patients with benign paroxysmal positional vertigo are usually safe to drive unless they are sensitive to horizontal head movements, in which case they should be advised not to drive until their condition has subsided or responded to treatment.

12.3.3   Chronic bilateral vestibular hypofunction

Most patients with fixed vestibular hypofunction are safe to drive because they have no acute attacks of vertigo. Those with complete bilateral absence of function may have more difficulty driving, particularly during evening hours or on bumpy roads, and may not be safe to drive.

Section 13
Cardiovascular diseases

Alert box

Unstable cardiac patients who require admission to hospital or intensified follow-up should cease driving immediately until they can be shown to be at an acceptably low risk.

13.1 Overview

These recommendations are based on the report of the Canadian Cardiovascular Society's 2003 Consensus Conference, *Assessment of the Cardiac Patient for Fitness to Drive and Fly*. They are intended to assist decision-makers in assessing the fitness of cardiac patients to drive and are not intended to diminish the role of the physician's clinical judgement in individual cases.

Recommendations are presented in tabular form. For definition of terms, see section 13.9. Details regarding these and other recommendations can be found in the full report.[*]

Please note:

- There are no prospective, controlled studies in which patients have been randomly chosen to be permitted or proscribed the driving privilege nor where patients have been randomly chosen to receive or not to receive physician advice not to drive.

- The defined standard of risk (see the "risk of harm" formula, Appendix F), while sensibly derived, is arbitrary and is not based on any evidence other than what has been acceptable historically.

- Given that all recommendations for driving eligibility are based on comparison with this arbitrary standard, they are based on expert opinion only.

- Application of the "risk of harm" formula throughout this section creates internal consistency among recommendations based on cardiovascular disorders, but does not imply consistency with recommendations based on other conditions or disorders, either in this guide or elsewhere.

- Wherever possible, best evidence was used to calculate the risks of driving, but the

---

[*] *Assessment of the cardiac patient for fitness to drive and fly: final report.* Ottawa: Canadian Cardiovascular Society; 2003. Available: www.ccs.ca/download/consensus_conference/consensus_conference_archives/2003_Fitness.pdf (accessed 4 Sept. 2006).

evidence itself does not support or deny driving licence restrictions for cardiac patients nor the mandatory reporting of such patients by their physicians.

13.2   Coronary artery disease

Most patients with coronary artery disease (CAD) pose a low risk to other road users while driving. However, certain conditions require careful evaluation and judgement. It seems fair to conclude on both clinical and physiologic grounds that the cardiovascular workload imposed by driving a vehicle is very light, and the risk that driving will provoke a recurrent acute coronary syndrome incident causing incapacitation is extremely small. Although a small percentage of acute coronary syndromes will present with sudden cardiac incapacitation, it is not possible with contemporary risk stratification to select these patients in a meaningful way.

13.2.1   Acute coronary syndromes

	Private driving	Commercial driving
ST elevation MI	1 month after discharge	3 months after discharge
Non-ST elevation MI with significant LV damage*	1 month after discharge	3 months after discharge
Non-ST elevation MI with minor LV damage*		
- If PCI performed during initial hospital stay	48 h after PCI	7 days after PCI
- If PCI not performed during initial hospital stay	7 days after discharge	30 days after discharge
Acute coronary syndrome without MI (unstable angina)		
- If PCI performed during initial hospital stay	48 h after PCI	7 days after PCI
- If PCI not performed during initial hospital stay	7 days after discharge	30 days after discharge

*Minor LV damage is classified as an MI defined only by elevated troponin with or without ECG changes and in the absence of a new wall motion abnormality. Significant LV damage is defined as any MI that is not classified as minor.

Note: ECG = electrocardiogram; LV = left ventricle; MI = myocardial infarction; PCI = percutaneous coronary intervention.

Notwithstanding any of the above recommendations, angiographic demonstration of 50% or greater reduction in the diameter of the left main coronary artery should disqualify the patient from commercial driving, and 70% or greater should disqualify the patient from private driving, unless treated with revascularization.

13.2.2   Stable coronary artery disease

	Private driving	Commercial driving
Stable angina	No restrictions	No restrictions
Asymptomatic CAD	No restrictions	No restrictions
PCI	48 h after PCI	7 days after PCI

Note: CAD = coronary artery disease; PCI = percutaneous coronary intervention.

13.2.3   Cardiac surgery for coronary artery disease

	Private driving	Commercial driving
CABG surgery	1 month after discharge	3 months after discharge

Note: CABG = coronary artery bypass graft.

13.3   Cardiac rhythm, arrhythmia devices and procedures

The general trend away from electrophysiology-study-guided risk stratification and toward risk stratification based on left ventricular function is reflected in the new guidelines, as the majority of implantable cardioverter defibrillator trials have identified left ventricular function as one of the most important determinants of risk.

13.3.1   Ventricular arrhythmias

	Private driving	Commercial driving
VF (no reversible cause)	6 months after event	Disqualified
Hemodynamically unstable VT	6 months after event	Disqualified
VT or VF due to a reversible cause*	No driving until/unless successful treatment of underlying condition	
Sustained VT with no associated impairment of consciousness; LVEF < 35%	3 months after event	Disqualified
Sustained VT with no impairment of consciousness; LVEF ≥ 35%; ICD has not been recommended	4 weeks after event satisfactory control	3 months after event satisfactory control
Nonsustained VT with no associated impairment of consciousness	No restriction	No restriction

*Examples include, but are not limited to, VF within 24 h of myocardial infarction, VF during coronary angiography, VF with electrocution, VF

cont'd

secondary to drug toxicity. Reversible cause VF recommendations overrule the VF recommendations if the reversible cause is treated successfully and the VF does not recur.

Note: ICD = implantable cardioverter defibrillator; LVEF = left ventricular ejection fraction; VF = ventricular fibrillation; VT = ventricular tachycardia.

13.3.2 *Paroxysmal supraventricular tachycardia, atrial fibrillation or atrial flutter*

	Private driving	Commercial driving
With impaired level of consciousness	Satisfactory control	Satisfactory control
Without impaired level of consciousness	No restriction	No restriction

Drivers should receive chronic anticoagulation if clinically indicated (i.e., in presence of atrial fibrillation or atrial flutter).

13.3.3 *Persistent or permanent atrial fibrillation or atrial flutter*

	Private driving	Commercial driving
Adequate ventricular rate control; no impaired level of consciousness	No restriction; chronic anticoagulation if clinically indicated	

13.3.4 *Sinus node dysfunction*

	Private driving	Commercial driving
No associated symptoms	No restriction	No restriction
Associated symptoms (sick sinus syndrome)	Disqualified until successful treatment	

13.3.5 *Atrioventricular and intraventricular block*

	Private driving	Commercial driving
Isolated first degree AV block Isolated RBBB Isolated left anterior fascicular block Isolated left posterior fascicular block	No restriction	
LBBB Bifascicular block Second degree AV block; Mobitz I First degree AV block + bifascicular block	Fit to drive if no associated impairment of level of consciousness	Fit to drive if no associated impairment of level of consciousness; and no higher grade AV block on an annual 24-h Holter

cont'd

Second degree AV block; Mobitz II (distal AV block) Alternating LBBB and RBBB Acquired third degree AV block	Disqualified	
Congenital third degree AV block	Fit to drive if no associated impairment of level of consciousness	Fit to drive if no associated impairment of level of consciousness; QRS duration ≤110 ms; and no documented pauses ≥ 3 seconds on an annual 24-h Holter

Note: AV = atrioventricular; LBBB = left bundle branch block; RBBB = right bundle branch block.

If a permanent pacemaker is implanted, the recommendations in section 13.3.6 prevail.

13.3.6 Permanent pacemakers

	Private driving	Commercial driving
All patients with a permanent pacemaker	• Waiting period 1 week after implant	• Waiting period 1 month after implant
	• No impaired level of consciousness after implant	• No impaired level of consciousness after implant
	• Normal sensing and capture on ECG	• Normal sensing and capture on ECG
	• No evidence of pacemaker malfunction at regular pacemaker clinic checks	• No evidence of pacemaker malfunction at regular pacemaker clinic checks

Note: ECG = electrocardiogram.

13.3.7 Implantable cardioverter defibrillators

	Private driving	Commercial driving
Primary prophylaxis; NYHA Classes I-III	4 weeks after implant	Disqualified*
A primary prophylaxis ICD has been recommended but declined by the patient	No restriction	Disqualified*
Secondary prophylaxis for VF or VT with decreased level of consciousness; NYHA Classes I-III	6 months after event†	Disqualified*
Secondary prophylaxis for sustained VT with no associated impairment of consciousness; NYHA Classes I-III	1 week post implant, in addition to the appropriate waiting period for the VT (see Section 13.3.1)	Disqualified*

cont'd

Any event resulting in device therapies being delivered (shock or ATP), in which level of consciousness was impaired or the therapy(ies) delivered by the device was/were disabling	Additional 6-month restriction	Disqualified*

*ICDs may sometimes be implanted in low-risk patients. Individual cases may be made for allowing a commercial driver to continue driving with an ICD provided the annual risk of sudden incapacitation is felt to be 1% or less.

†The 6-month period begins not at the time of ICD implant, but rather at the time of the last documented episode of sustained symptomatic VT, or syncope judged to be likely due to VT or cardiac arrest.

Note: ATP = antitachycardia pacing; ICD = implantable cardioverter defibrillator; NYHA = New York Heart Association; VF = ventricular fibrillation; VT = ventricular tachycardia.

For patients who have a bradycardia indication for pacing as well, the additional criteria under Section 13.3.6 also apply.

All patients must be followed from a technical standpoint in a device clinic with appropriate expertise.

13.3.8   Other

	Private driving	Commercial driving
Brugada's syndrome; long QT syndrome; arrhythmogenic right ventricular cardiomyopathy (ARVC)	• Appropriate investigation and treatment guided by a cardiologist • 6 months after any event causing impaired level of consciousness	Disqualified*
Catheter ablation procedure	48 h after discharge	1 week after discharge
EPS with no inducible sustained ventricular arrhythmias	48 h after discharge	1 week after discharge

*Inherited heart diseases may sometimes be identified to pose a very low risk to patients. Individual cases may be made for allowing a commercial driver to continue driving despite the diagnosis of one of these diseases, provided the annual risk of sudden incapacitation is felt to be 1% or less.

Note: EPS = electrophysiology study.

13.4   Syncope

Most episodes of syncope represent vasovagal syncope, which can usually be diagnosed by history and do not warrant further investigation. When syncope is unexplained, further testing is necessary to arrive at a diagnosis and direct possible therapy. Because there is a small risk of recurrence and incapacitation during driving, consideration of restriction of privileges is intuitive to protect both the patient and the public.

A patient with structural heart disease (reduced ejection fraction, previous myocardial infarction, significant congenital heart disease) is potentially high risk and should undergo driving restriction pending clarification of underlying heart disease and etiology of syncope. It is well known that syncope, a previous aborted cardiac arrest, one or more episodes of sustained ventricular tachycardia (VT) and a history of sudden death in young family members are strong indicators of a high risk of sudden death.

	Private driving	Commercial driving
Single episode of typical vasovagal syncope*	No restriction	
Diagnosed and treated cause, (e.g., permanent pacemaker for bradycardia)	Wait 1 week	Wait 1 month
Reversible cause (e.g., hemorrhage, dehydration)	Successful treatment of underlying condition	
Situational syncope with avoidable trigger, (e.g., micturition syncope, defecation syncope)	Wait 1 week	
• Single episode of unexplained syncope • Recurrent vasovagal syncope (within 12 months)	Wait 1 week	Wait 12 months
Recurrent episode of unexplained syncope (within 12 months)	Wait 3 months	Wait 12 months
Syncope due to documented tachyarrhythmia, or inducible tachyarrhythmia at EPS	Refer to section 13.3.1	

*No restriction is recommended unless the syncope occurs in the sitting position, or if it is determined that there may be an insufficient prodrome to pilot the vehicle to the roadside to a stop before losing consciousness. If vasovagal syncope is atypical, the restrictions for "unexplained" syncope apply.

Note: EPS = electrophysiology study.

13.5   Valvular heart disease

Valvular heart disease can range from mild to severe. In general, the risk posed to the public by a driver with valvular disease depends largely on

•   symptomatic status

•   echocardiography data that quantify both the valvular lesion as well as left ventricular dimensions

13.5.1   Medically treated valvular heart disease

	Private driving	Commercial driving
Aortic stenosis	• NYHA Class I or II • No episodes of impaired level of consciousness	• Asymptomatic • NYHA Class I • AVA ≥ 1.0 cm^2 • EF $\geq 35\%$

cont'd

| Aortic regurgitation
Mitral stenosis
Mitral regurgitation | • No episodes of impaired level of consciousness
• NYHA Class I or II | • No episodes of impaired level of consciousness
• NYHA Class I
• EF ≥ 35% |

Note: AVA = aortic valve area; EF = ejection fraction; NYHA = New York Heart Association.

13.5.2   Surgically treated valvular heart disease

	Private driving	Commercial driving
Mechanical prostheses Mitral bioprostheses with non-sinus rhythm Mitral valve repair with non-sinus rhythm	• 6 weeks after discharge • No thromboembolic complications • On anticoagulant therapy	• 3 months after discharge • No thromboembolic complications • Anticoagulant therapy • NYHA Class I • EF ≥ 35%
Aortic bioprostheses Mitral bioprostheses with sinus rhythm Mitral valve repair with sinus rhythm	• 6 weeks after discharge • No thromboembolic complications	• 3 months after discharge • No thromboembolic complications • NYHA Class I • EF ≥ 35%

Note: EF = ejection fraction; NYHA = New York Heart Association.

13.6   Congestive heart failure, left ventricular dysfunction, cardiomyopathy, transplantation

Patients with cardiomyopathy, with or without a history of heart failure, potentially pose a risk on the roads. Functional status is a major determinant of fitness, as is the left ventricular ejection fraction. Because sudden death is so common in this group, physicians are encouraged to cross-reference this section with section 13.3, Cardiac rhythm, arrythmia devices and procedures. In the event of a conflict, the more restrictive recommendation applies.

	Private driving	Commercial driving
NYHA Class I	No restriction	EF ≥ 35%
NYHA Class II	No restriction	EF ≥ 35%
NYHA Class III	No restriction	Disqualified
NYHA Class IV Receiving intermittent outpatient or home inotropes Left ventricular assist device	Disqualified	

cont'd

Heart transplant	• 6 weeks after discharge • NYHA Class I or II • On stable immunotherapy • Annual assessment	• 6 months after discharge • Annual assessment • EF ≥ 35% • NYHA Class I • Annual non-invasive test of ischemic burden showing no evidence of active ischemia

Note: EF = ejection fraction; NYHA = New York Heart Association.

13.7 Hypertrophic cardiomyopathy

	Private driving	**Commercial driving**
All patients with hypertophic cardiomyopathy	No episodes of impaired level of consciousness	• LV wall thickness < 30 mm • No history of syncope • No NSVT on annual Holter • No family history of sudden death at a young age • No BP decrease with exercise

Note: BP = blood pressure; LV = left ventricle; NSVT: nonsustained ventricular tachycardia.

13.8 Cardiac rehabilitation programs

Cardiac rehabilitation programs are uniquely positioned to evaluate patients with respect to symptom status and fitness to drive.

Patients within cardiac rehabilitation programs include those with

- coronary artery disease including people with angina and a history of mechanical revascularization (coronary artery bypass surgery or percutaneous coronary interventions)
- cardiac rhythm disturbances
- pacemakers
- syncope
- valvular heart disease
- congenital heart disease
- hypertrophic cardiomyopathy
- left ventricular systolic dysfunction, congestive heart failure or both
- previous cardiac transplantation.

13.9 Definitions

NYHA functional classification:

- Class I: Patients with cardiac disease but without resulting limitation of physical activity.

Ordinary physical activity does not cause undue fatigue, palpitation, dyspnea or anginal pain.

- Class II: Patients with cardiac disease resulting in slight limitation of physical activity. They are comfortable at rest. Ordinary physical activity results in fatigue, palpitation, dyspnea or anginal pain.
- Class III: Patients with cardiac disease resulting in marked limitation of physical activity. They are comfortable at rest. Less than ordinary activity causes fatigue, palpitation, dyspnea or anginal pain.
- Class IV: Patients with cardiac disease resulting in inability to carry on any physical activity without discomfort. Symptoms of heart failure or anginal syndrome may be present even at rest. If any physical activity is undertaken, discomfort increases.

Waiting period: The time interval following onset of a disqualifying cardiac condition, initiation of a stable program of medical therapy or performance of a therapeutic procedure (whichever is applicable) during which driving should generally be disallowed for medical reasons.

- Recurrence of the disqualifying condition or circumstance during this time resets the waiting period.
- If more than one waiting period would apply, the longer one should be used, except where stated otherwise.

Satisfactory control (for supraventricular tachycardia, atrial fibrillation or atrial flutter, which are associated with cerebral ischemia):

- Supraventricular tachycardia — Successful radiofrequency ablation of the substrate, plus an appropriate waiting period (see section 13.3.2); or a 3-month waiting period on medical therapy with no recurrence of SVT associated with cerebral ischemia during this time.
- Atrial fibrillation or atrial flutter — A 3-month waiting period after appropriate treatment during which there are no recurrences of symptoms associated with cerebral ischemia. If atrial fibrillation is treated with AV node ablation and pacemaker implantation, or if atrial flutter is treated successfully with an isthmus ablation (with proven establishment of bidirectional isthmus block), then the waiting periods in section 13.3.2 apply.
- Sustained ventricular tachycardia with a left ventricular ejection fraction greater than or equal to 40% and no associated cerebral ischemia — Successful ablation of the substrate plus a 1-week waiting period, or pharmacologic treatment plus the waiting period specified in section 13.3.1.

Sustained ventricular tachycardia: Ventricular tachycardia having a cycle length of 500 milliseconds (ms) or less and lasting 30 seconds or more or causing hemodynamic collapse

Nonsustained ventricular tachycardia: Ventricular tachycardia ≥ 3 beats; having a cycle length of 500 ms or less and lasting less than 30 seconds; without hemodynamic collapse.

13.10   Abnormal blood pressure

13.10.1 Hypertension
Hypertension, other than uncontrolled malignant hypertension, is not by itself a contraindication to the operation of any class of motor vehicle, although the complications that can arise from increased blood pressure such as cardiac, ocular or renal damage may well preclude safe driving. Sustained hypertension above 170/110 mmHg is, however, often accompanied by complications that make driving dangerous and these patients must be evaluated carefully.

Higher standards are required of commercial drivers than of private drivers. If a commercial driver is found to have a blood pressure of 170/110 mmHg or higher, the investigation must include an electrocardiogram, chest radiography, fundoscopic examination and measurement of blood urea nitrogen (BUN). If there is a marked deviation from norm, the patient should be referred to an internist for an opinion.

The long-term risks associated with sustained hypertension (over 170/110 mmHg) are such that patients who are unable to reduce their blood pressure to a level below this figure should not be recommended for licensing as commercial drivers.

13.10.2 Hypotension
Hypotension is not a contraindication to the operation of any type of motor vehicle unless it has caused episodes of syncope. If syncope has occurred, the patient should discontinue driving. If it is possible to prevent further attacks by treatment, it is then safe to resume driving a private vehicle, but not heavy transport or commercial vehicles.

13.11 Anticoagulants
Although the use of anticoagulant drugs is not by itself a contraindication to driving any class of motor vehicle, the underlying condition that led to prescribing the anticoagulant may be incompatible with safe driving.

Section 14
Cerebrovascular diseases (including stroke) and traumatic brain injury

> **Alert box**
> Patients who have experienced either a single or recurrent transient ischemic attack should not drive a motor vehicle until a medical assessment is completed.

14.1   Overview

Cerebrovascular disease, as well as traumatic brain injury and acquired brain injury can cause symptoms that can lead to unsafe driving yet are difficult to detect (e.g., visual field defects). A careful history and physical examination, including an assessment of insight and judgement, are important. If a problem that may affect driving is suspected, then a comprehensive driver evaluation is the most practical method of determining fitness to drive. Where resources are available, assessment by a trained occupational therapist would be optimal. A motor vehicle licensing authority road test can be helpful in assessing functional capacity to drive. However, it cannot always be relied on to reveal the true extent of the disability, both because of the fluctuating nature of the symptoms and the examiner's inability to evaluate all potentially related physical and cognitive issues.

14.2   Transient ischemic attacks

The abrupt onset of a partial loss of neurologic function during a transient ischemic attack (TIA) persisting for less than 24 hours and clearing without residual signs should not be ignored in anyone who drives a motor vehicle as it raises the possibility of a later stroke. After the first warning symptoms, patients have a 5%–6% chance of a stroke annually. The risk is generally accepted as 10% (absolute) for the group as a whole and is as high as 30% for some patients based on clinical and imaging indicators. Evidence indicates that there is a substantial risk of recurrence during the first 3 months after the TIA.

Patients who have experienced either a single or recurrent TIA should not be allowed to drive any type of motor vehicle until a medical assessment and appropriate investigations are completed. They may resume driving if the neurologic assessment discloses no residual loss of functional ability, and any underlying cause has been addressed with appropriate treatment.

14.3   Cerebrovascular accidents

14.3.1   Brain aneurysms

Symptomatic cerebral aneurysms that have not been surgically repaired are an absolute contradiction to driving any class of motor vehicle. Following successful treatment, the patient may drive a vehicle for which a regular licence is required (i.e., Class 5, 6, etc.) after a symptom-free period of 3 months. The patient will be eligible to drive commercial vehicles after being symptom free for 6 months. Any symptoms of physical, psychologic or cognitive skills should be evaluated for significance, the patient cautioned not to drive and the condition reported to the licensing authority

Table 3: Recommendations for patients with symptomatic cerebral aneurysm

Patient condition	Private driving	Commercial driving
Untreated cerebral aneurysm	Disqualified	Disqualified
After surgical treatment	Symptom free for 3 months	Symptom free for 6 months

14.3.2   Stroke

Patients who have had a stroke should not drive for at least 1 month. During this time they require assessment by their regular physician. They may resume driving if
- the physician notes no clinically significant motor, cognitive, perceptual or vision deficits
- neurologic assessment discloses no obvious risk of sudden recurrence
- any underlying cause has been addressed with appropriate treatment and
- a post stroke seizure has not occurred in the interim.

Any available information from the patient's treating occupational therapist, physiotherapist or speech pathologist should be reviewed to assist with the determination of deficits that may not be visible or detected during an office visit.

Where there is a residual loss of motor power, a driving evaluation at a designated driver assessment centre may be required (see Appendix E). The driver assessment centre can make recommendations for driving equipment or modification strategies such as use of a steering wheel "spinner knob" or left-foot gas pedal. Training in the safe use of the equipment should be provided.

The physician should take particular care to note any changes in personality, alertness, insight (executive functions) and decision-making ability in stroke patients, however subtle and inconsistent. These types of changes could significantly affect driving ability. The physician may be assisted by reports from reliable family members in discerning whether the patient's judgement and awareness are altered in day-to-day activities. These patients may drive well one day, but incompetently the next. Patients with a right-brain stroke may be verbally quite intact but very much impaired with regard to their insight, judgement and perceptual skills. Such patients may even be reported for erratic driving but could do quite well on a standard driving road test. Patients with a left-brain stroke frequently present with some degree of aphasia. Although aphasia is not an absolute contraindication to safe driving, it requires the physician's attention and further evaluation.

Patients who sustain a visual field deficit from the stroke require a visual field study completed by an optometrist or ophthalmologist. The report should be sent to the motor vehicle licensing authority. All changes in visual field must be reported to the licensing authority who will then provide direction to the driver as to what steps he or she will need to take. Although a visual field deficit is no longer considered to be an absolute contraindication to safe driving, each jurisdiction has its own particular assessment to further evaluate this condition.

Patients who have had a stroke and subsequently resume driving should remain under regular medical supervision, as the episode may be the forerunner of a gradual decline in their thinking processes (e.g., multi-infarct dementia). Although sometimes the denial of expressway or high-speed driving privileges or limiting driving to areas familiar to the driver may be all that is required, such restrictions are not enforceable within the majority of licensing authorities and there is little evidence demonstrating that restricted licensing improves driving safety after a stroke.

14.4   Traumatic and acquired brain injury

The apparent severity of the original traumatic event may not correlate with the degree of persisting cognitive dysfunction post-injury. There is also often great variability in recovery; individuals with severe injury may have minor persisting deficits and, in contrast, those with mild brain injury may have significant persisting deficits. Multiple cognitive and physical impairments, including changes in reaction time and visual-motor processing, commonly occur following traumatic brain injury (TBI) and can impair ability to drive. The same is true for acquired brain injuries, which can occur as a result of anoxia, prolonged hypoglycemia or other cerebral insults.

For patients experiencing post-traumatic seizures, see section 10.7.1.

14.4.1 Immediate injury assessment

To drive safely, TBI survivors require insight into their disability, as well as
- adequate reaction times
- adequate ability to coordinate visual-motor function (for steering)

- adequate leg function for braking (or ability to use adaptive technology)
- adequate ability to divide attention to perform multiple simultaneous tasks
- enough responsibility to comply reliably with the rules of the road and to drive within any conditions set by licensing authorities.

Knowledge about the effects of TBI, a careful history, information from family or other reliable informants and additional cognitive screening will help the physician make the best decisions. If cognitive or significant physical deficits are found, consider referral for rehabilitation assessment.

Generally, individuals with moderate to severe TBI (Glasgow coma score < 13, or requirement for admission to hospital for treatment of TBI) will often require comprehensive assessment.

Most people with "mild" TBI will improve spontaneously. However, they should be monitored for symptoms. A significant proportion (10%–15%) may require further assessment. Implications for driving should be considered routinely.

For all patients who have had a TBI, a driving history should be done and included as part of the medical record. Topics to include are

- Does the patient have a valid licence (registration number and expiry date)?
- What classification and conditions are attached to the licence?
- How long has he or she been driving?
- Has he or she received any professional driving instruction?
- Describe any crash in which he or she was the driver.
    - Did any of these crashes result in injury, including possible TBI?
    - Were alcohol, drugs or prescription medications a factor?
    - Was he or she agitated or combative just after the crash?
    - Was he or she staring or showing a delayed response to conversation with others?
    - Is there a difference between the family's and the injured person's observations about his or her behaviour since the crash?

If there were observations of the patient appearing confused immediately after the crash, even if only for a brief period, or if symptoms of concussion are evident, the patient should be advised not to drive until medically cleared to do so. If alcohol, drugs or prescription medications were a factor, the evidence supports screening for a substance use disorder. With the patient's consent, a family member should also be notified, and it is preferable to document the name of the physician who will be responsible for this review and when it will occur.

14.4.2 Long-term injury assessment

Symptoms: The following symptoms, when they occur shortly after the trauma and then persist, may indicate residual disability:

- becoming fatigued easily
- disordered sleep
- headache
- vertigo, dizziness or balance problems
- unprovoked irritability or aggression
- anxiety, depression or affective lability
- changes in personality
- apathy or lack of spontaneity
- short-term memory impairment
- decreased tolerance for stress and adverse effects of medication
- decreased sense of smell (often experienced as not being able to enjoy the taste of food)
- trouble reading others' emotions
- difficulty knowing if something is intended to be humorous or not
- executive function changes (difficulty planning and performing complex tasks).

Visual field defects that may follow TBI include a clinical history of bumping into things on one side or of "neglect" on one side. These may be the first sign of an undiagnosed homonymous hemianopsia.

History and physical: The TBI survivor often has poor insight and awareness of the acquired deficits. The role of self-awareness of deficits is central in determining whether an individual with residual deficits may be able to drive safely. Collateral history is essential, as the TBI patient may lack insight. Appearing confused immediately after the crash and injury, or any period of amnesia confirmed by observers, is a risk factor for persistent cognitive disability, even if the Glasgow coma scale in the emergency department is 15/15. Because of the complexities of brain function and the specialized function of some areas, one cognitive skill may be spared by the injury, while another is impaired or lost.

A history and physical are not enough to assess fitness to drive after TBI adequately when any signs of concussion or brain injury have been evident. Standard neurologic examination cannot always determine the presence or absence of cognitive dysfunction after TBI. In these cases, additional objective information is useful to support opinion.

In addition to the standard visual acuity requirements, a minimal assessment should include
- visual field testing
- cognitive screening to assess memory, attention, reaction time, visual perception and visual-motor skills.

Investigations: Although it may be possible to confirm the presence of diffuse axonal injury with specialized MRI scans, it is important to realize that full functional recovery may follow clearly abnormal computed tomography scans. Conversely, persistent cognitive dysfunction is seen in some individuals after apparently normal neuro-imaging investigations.

14.5   Functional impairment

The lack of consensus on measurement of cognitive indicators and ability indices continues to make this a problematic issue. If medical assessment alone is not sufficient to determine driving suitability, then further evaluation by medical specialists, neuropsychologic testing or formal comprehensive driving assessment may give a more accurate evaluation and help to develop a better understanding of specific driving problems.

Even when comprehensive rehabilitation facilities are not readily available, there are some things that the treating physician can do. For example, physicians can use a standardized screening questionnaire for the assessment of concussion, such as those used in sports medicine.

Section 15
Vascular diseases

15.1   Overview

The presence of an aortic aneurysm or deep venous thrombosis is the main concern with respect to fitness to drive.

15.2   Arterial aneurysm

An arterial aneurysm is potentially dangerous if it is expanding and there is a possibility of sudden rupture. The physician should document maximum aneurysm diameter using an appropriate test when completing a medical examination report for the motor vehicle licensing authority. An abdominal ultrasound examination or computed tomography scan will reliably determine the size of the aneurysm. Only the anterior-posterior or transverse diameter is predictive of rupture; the length of the aneurysm has no relation to rupture. Ongoing review of the patient is required. A patient with an aortic aneurysm should have the benefit of the opinion of a vascular surgeon.

Currently, it is generally accepted that aneurysms < 5 cm transverse or anterior-posterior diameter have a lower than 1% annual risk of rupture. In men, for aneurysms > 6 cm, the risk of rupture exceeds 10% in 1 year if left untreated. Currently, men with aneurysms > 5.5 cm are evaluated for repair and may undergo surgery depending on comorbid conditions. For women, aneurysm repair is considered for those > 5 cm.

Thus, the decision to license drivers with aneurysms larger than the currently accepted thresholds for repair should consider aneurysm size and the patient's comorbid conditions. In selected cases, the comorbid conditions and the threat of aneurysm rupture secondary to size (> 6 cm in men and > 5.5 cm in women) may preclude driving.

Following successful open or endovascular aneurysm repair, the patient may drive assuming that no other medical contraindication exists.

Thoracic and thoracoabdominal aneurysm rupture is also related to aneurysm size. Prospective data comparing early surgery to conservative follow-up are not available. The threshold for repair of thoracic and thoracoabdominal aneurysms is influenced by size, extent and location of these aneurysms. Therefore, definitive recommendations await prospective data.

15.3 Peripheral arterial vascular diseases

Raynaud's phenomenon, Buerger's disease and atherosclerotic occlusions, if of sufficient severity to cause symptoms, require evaluation. They rarely preclude driving but require ongoing surveillance.

15.4 Diseases of the veins

Patients with acute episodes of deep venous thrombosis are at risk of pulmonary embolization. Physicians should advise patients with acute deep venous thrombosis to refrain from driving. Following the institution of appropriate treatment, a patient may safely resume driving any type of motor vehicle.

Section 16
Respiratory diseases

16.1   Overview

Some respiratory diseases may, if severe enough, interfere with the safe operation of a motor vehicle. A decrease in the provision of oxygen to the brain could impair judgement, reduce concentration and slow response times. Marked dyspnea may also limit physical ability to operate a motor vehicle.

16.2   Assessment

Impairment associated with dyspnea can be characterized as

• **Mild** — Dyspnea when walking quickly on level ground or when walking uphill; ability to keep pace with people of same age and body build walking on level ground, but not on hills or stairs.

• **Moderate** — Shortness of breath when walking for a few minutes or after 100 m walking on level ground.

• **Severe** — Too breathless to leave the house, breathless when dressing. The presence of untreated respiratory failure.

16.3   Chronic obstructive pulmonary disease (COPD) and other chronic respiratory diseases

Driving could be dangerous for a patient with untreated chronic hypoxia. Many patients with chronic respiratory diseases, such as COPD, drive safely and regularly, even when oxygen use is required. A driving assessment, road test or both are recommended if the physician has any doubt. Oxygen equipment must be safely secured in the vehicle.

Table 4: Recommendations for patients with chronic respiratory disease

Level of impairment	Private driving	Commercial driving
None or mild	No restrictions	No restrictions
Moderate	No restrictions	Depends on the nature of the activities. May require road testing.
Moderate or severe, plus supplemental oxygen at rest	Road test, while using supplemental oxygen. Equipment must be secured safely. Annual clinical assessment required.	Disqualified

16.4   Permanent tracheostomy

A person with a permanent tracheostomy who has no difficulty keeping the opening clear of mucous should be able to drive any class of motor vehicle, provided that the medical condition which made the tracheostomy necessary does not preclude driving.

See also section 23.3, under Motorcycles and off-road vehicles.

Section 17
Endocrine and metabolic disorders

Alert box
- In severe cases, many endocrine or metabolic diseases, treated or untreated, may impair judgement, motor skills or level of consciousness. If these factors are present or are likely to occur, then the patient should be advised not to drive until the medical condition is stabilized.
- A hypoglycemic episode severe enough to require the intervention of a third party is an immediate contraindication to driving.

17.1   Overview
Disturbances in the functioning of the endocrine glands may be the source of many symptoms with a wide range of severity. Patients with suspected or confirmed endocrine disorders should always be carefully evaluated to make certain that their symptoms do not make them unsafe drivers. The endocrine and metabolic conditions discussed below are among the most common ones that physicians may be called on to assess because of their potential for interfering with driving safety. Fitness to drive must be assessed on a case-by-case basis as the range of signs and symptoms is highly variable.

17.2   Diabetes mellitus
Advances in treatment, medical technology and self-monitoring have increased the ability of patients with diabetes to control their disease and operate a motor vehicle safely. Fitness of these patients to drive must be assessed on a case-by-case basis. Patients with diabetes should be encouraged to take an active role in assessing their ability to drive by maintaining personal health records and accurate blood-glucose monitoring logs. Patients should have information concerning avoidance, recognition and appropriate therapeutic intervention for hypoglycemia. The annual medical examination of a driver with diabetes should always include a full review of possible complications to exclude eye disease, neuropathy (autonomic, sensory, motor), renal disease and cardiovascular and cerebrovascular disease of a degree that would

preclude issuing the class of licence requested. Cumulative diabetic complications may cause functional impairment requiring evaluation above and beyond what might be required for any specific level of complication or level of glycemic control. In general, a patient is considered fit to drive if it can be demonstrated that he or she is fastidious and knowledgeable about controlling his or her blood-glucose levels and able to avoid severe hypoglycemic episodes.

The recommendations below are based on the *Canadian Diabetes Association's Clinical Practice Guidelines for Diabetes and Private and Commercial Driving* (2003), and *Canadian Diabetes Association 2003 Clinical Practice Guidelines for the Prevention and Management of Diabetes in Canada*, both available at www.diabetes.ca. The recommendations are presented in both tabular and textual format.

	Private drivers	**Commercial drivers**
Diabetes that is controlled without medications or treated with metformin, acarbose or thiazoledinediones	These patients are at very low risk for severe hypoglycemia. Patients must have no complications of diabetes that may impair their ability to drive including eye disease, renal disease, neuropathy (autonomic, sensory or motor) and cardiovascular disease.	
Diabetes treated by insulin secretagogues (sulfonyl-ureas, repaglinide, nateglinide)	These patients are generally at a low risk for severe hypoglycemia Patients should be encouraged to wear a medical bracelet. Patients may usually drive *all types of vehicles* if they • have a good understanding of their condition • follow instructions about diet, medication and prevention of hypoglycemia. • remain under regular medical supervision Patients must have no complications of diabetes that may impair their ability to drive including eye disease, renal disease, neuropathy (autonomic, sensory or motor) cerebrovascular and cardiovascular disease.	
Diabetes treated with insulin	Patients should wear a medical bracelet Patients may drive if they • are under regular medical supervision • understand their diabetic condition and the close interrelations among	See Canadian Diabetes Association guidelines listed in section 17.2.2 for initial application, exclusion criteria, annual recertification and driving

cont'd

insulin and diet and exercise
- follow their physician's advice
- demonstrate appropriate management of hypoglycemia
- have no history of severe hypoglycemic episodes in the last 6 months while awake
- have followed CDA glucose monitoring guidelines if previous hypoglycemia unawareness or severe hypoglycemia.

Patients must have no complications of diabetes that may impair their ability to drive including eye disease, renal disease, neuropathy (autonomic, sensory or motor) cardiovascular disease and cerebrovascular disease.

17.2.1   *Diabetes not treated with insulin*

Patients with diabetes that is well controlled by diet alone or with such medications as metformin, acarbose and thiazoledinediones have a very low risk of hypoglycemia. These patients may drive all vehicles with relative safety.

Patients with diabetes that is treated by a combination of diet and oral medications, such as sulfonlyureas, repaglinide and nateglinide, are at low risk of a severe hypoglycemic reaction. They can usually drive all types of motor vehicles with relative safety provided

- They have a good understanding of their condition.
- They follow their physician's instructions about diet, medication, blood-glucose monitoring and the prevention of hypoglycemia.
- They remain under regular medical supervision to ensure that any progression in their condition or development of complications does not go undetected.

17.2.2   *Diabetes treated with insulin*

Private drivers: Patients who require insulin to control their diabetes can drive private vehicles if

- They are under the regular medical supervision of their physician.
- They understand their diabetic condition and the close interrelations among insulin, diet and exercise.

- They conscientiously follow their physician's advice, particularly about diet, exercise, blood-glucose monitoring, the prevention and management of hypoglycemia and weight control.

Patients with a history of severe hypoglycemic episodes should not drive until they have re-established stable glycemic control (usually 6 months, but the period must be evaluated on a case-by-case basis). Severe hypoglycemia is defined as a hypoglycemic reaction that requires outside intervention to abort or that produces an alteration in level or loss of consciousness. Drivers with hypoglycemia unawareness or previous severe hypoglycemia should follow Canadian Diabetes Association glucose monitoring guidelines.

Commercial drivers: Commercial drivers, especially those who operate heavy trucks over long distances, can have great difficulty maintaining the essential balance between insulin dose, food intake and physical exertion because they are often required to work long and irregular hours, travel long distances in inclement weather and perform unexpected heavy physical labour, such as the application and removal of tire chains. To add to the problem, truck drivers are often unable to stop if they become ill while on duty, even though an acute illness can make it difficult for them to keep their diabetic condition under proper control. Their mealtimes may frequently be delayed and meals may occasionally be missed altogether.

The Canadian Diabetes Association recommends that people with diabetes treated with insulin, who hold commercial licences, observe the following guidelines on the initial application, exclusion, annual medical recertification and driving.

Guidelines on initial application for a commercial licence
- The applicant must undergo a complete assessment with an internist or specialist in diabetes care or, in special circumstances, a family physician trained in diabetes care. The applicant should have available medical records for the preceding 24 months.
- The applicant must supply evidence of attendance at a diabetes education program.
- The applicant must receive a complete physical examination including a full eye examination by an ophthalmologist or optometrist.
- Laboratory tests: a glycosylated hemoglobin (HbA_1C) test within the past 3 months.
- The applicant must have a log of blood-glucose measurements performed at least twice daily in the last 6 months or since diagnosis if onset of diabetes occurred within the last 6 months. A downloaded log from a memory-equipped glucose meter is preferred.

Exclusion criteria for a commercial licence
To continue driving the patient must have
- No episode of hypoglycemia within the previous 6 months requiring intervention by a

third party for correction, or producing loss of consciousness, even if spontaneous recovery occurred.
- No episodes of hypoglycemia appearing in the absence of warning symptoms ("hypoglycemia unawareness") unless there is documentation of recovery of warning symptoms at a later date.
- No instability of insulin treatment regimen. Unstable insulin regimen is defined as a significant change in, or the introduction of, insulin therapy. The patient should be considered as remaining in an unstable state for at least 1 month after a significant change in the number of injections or dose of insulin, or the introduction of insulin. He or she should be assessed monthly with respect to the occurrence of hypoglycemic episodes until the patient is believed to be on a stable insulin regimen.
- No significant new or worsening complications of diabetes.
- Evidence of adequate self-monitoring of blood glucose and knowledge of causes, symptoms and treatment of hypoglycemic reactions.

Guidelines for the annual medical recertification of insulin treated commercial drivers
All insulin-treated commercial drivers are required to have an annual medical examination and recertification. The required data include
- medical records for the past 12 months
- the results of a complete physical examination, including a full eye examination by an ophthalmologist or optometrist
- laboratory tests: 2 tests for HbA_1C at 3-month intervals
- log of blood-glucose measurements, preferably downloaded from a memory-equipped glucose meter, with record of the last 6 months.

The exclusion criteria are the same as for the initial application for a commercial licence. As well, the commercial driver should not be recertified if there is evidence of inadequate blood-glucose monitoring during driving or non-compliance with the driving guidelines listed below.

Guidelines for commercial driving
- Supplies required to be carried by the patient at all times while driving include
  - self-monitoring equipment
  - a source of rapidly absorbable glucose
  - syringes, pump or injector and insulin to maintain regular therapeutic regimen.
- Blood-glucose concentration must be tested within 1 hour before driving and approximately every 4 hours while driving. Driving should be stopped if glucose level falls below 6 mmol/L (108 mg/dL) and not resumed until glucose level has risen following food ingestion.

- The schedule of work to be adopted should be approved by the treating physician as compatible with the insulin regimen.

17.3   Nondiabetic renal glycosuria

Patients with nondiabetic renal glycosuria can safely drive any type of motor vehicle.

17.4   Nondiabetic hypoglycemia

Patients who become faint or unconscious from spontaneous episodes of hypoglycemia that is unrelated to diabetes cannot drive any type of vehicle safely and require immediate, accurate diagnosis and treatment of the condition. Those with milder symptoms, who have never lost consciousness or the ability to respond normally to external stimuli, can operate private vehicles without excessive risk. They should not drive passenger-carrying or commercial vehicles until this problem has been controlled.

17.5   Thyroid disease

17.5.1   Patients with hyperthyroidism

Patients with hyperthyroidism complicated by cardiac, neurologic or muscular symptoms that impair judgement or motor skills should not drive any type of motor vehicle until the condition has been controlled.

17.5.2   Patients with symptomatic hypothyroidism

Patients with symptomatic hypothyroidism that impairs judgement or motor skills should not drive any type of motor vehicle until the condition has been brought under satisfactory control.

17.6   Parathyroid disease

Patients with hypocalcemia with significant neurologic or muscular symptoms should not drive. If their symptoms respond well to treatment, they should be able to resume driving all vehicles without undue risk.

17.7   Pituitary disease

17.7.1   Posterior deficiency

Patients with diabetes insipidus should not drive commercial or passenger-carrying vehicles until their condition has been stabilized with treatment. It is safe for them to drive private motor vehicles under careful medical supervision unless disabling central nervous system symptoms or other significant symptoms develop.

17.7.2   Anterior deficiency

Patients with panhypopituitarism or other anterior pituitary hormone deficiencies may develop a number of symptoms that may impair their ability to drive a motor vehicle safely. They should not drive until their medical condition is assessed and treated. Patients with pituitary tumours or other space-occupying lesions should be regularly assessed for visual field defects.

17.7.3   Acromegaly

Patients with acromegaly, who have started to develop muscle weakness, pain, easy fatiguing, significant neurologic symptoms, visual disturbances, cardiac enlargement or intractable headaches should discontinue all driving. After treatment, and if vision is satisfactory and other symptoms do not significantly affect function, they should be able to resume all driving safely.

17.8   Adrenal disease

17.8.1   Cushing's disease

Patients with Cushing's disease (adrenal cortical hyperfunction) who have developed muscle weakness should be advised to stop driving. If they improve after treatment, they may resume driving all vehicles, but must remain under close medical supervision.

17.8.2   Addison's disease

A patient with Addison's disease (adrenal cortical hypofunction) may drive all vehicles provided the condition has been successfully treated and controlled and they remain under close medical supervision.

17.8.3   Pheochromocytoma

Hyperfunction of the adrenal medulla due to the development of a pheochromocytoma with headache, dizziness or blurred vision is a contraindication to the operation of any type of motor vehicle unless these symptoms are significantly relieved by treatment.

17.9   Obesity

A grossly obese driver may not be able to respond rapidly enough to a sudden emergency situation and may not be able to operate vehicle controls properly. If the examining physician believes that an obese patient might have difficulty driving safely or maintaining a vehicle, the physician should recommend a road test.

17.10   Hepatic encephalopathy

Patients with symptomatic hepatic encephalopathy should not be allowed to drive any type of motor vehicle.

Section 18
Renal diseases

> **Alert box**
>
> Dialysis patients should not drive if their scheduled dialysis treatment is delayed, or if they have a complicating medical problem that has not been assessed.

18.1   Overview

This section reviews issues associated with dialysis and renal transplantation. Patients with end-stage renal disease may be treated with facility-based or home hemodialysis, or home peritoneal dialysis. Most patients can continue to drive safely after adjusting to a stable dialysis regimen.

Patients on dialysis often develop concurrent medical problems or general debility that can lead to a temporary or permanent inability to drive safely. The attending physician should notify the licensing authority if any problems arise that could make driving hazardous, including a potentially short-term but serious change in health status, such as a systemic infection, significant electrolyte abnormality, ischemic coronary event or symptoms such as weakness or hypotension that occur while adjusting to a new dialysis regimen.

18.2   Dialysis

Patients with end-stage renal disease maintained on hemodialysis or peritoneal dialysis can drive any class of motor vehicle, provided they possess adequate cognitive and sensorimotor ability.

Drivers undertaking trips must take into account access to dialysis and supplies.

All commercial drivers must be under the supervision of a nephrologist or an internist and have an annual medical review. Commercial drivers must be able to receive appropriate dialysis therapy while performing their work. For patients undergoing peritoneal dialysis, adequate supplies and an appropriate physical environment for exchanges must always be available. Hemodialysis is generally not a feasible treatment modality for a long-distance driver. If a commercial driver is planning to travel significant distances from home, unexpected delays due to weather, highway conditions or demands of their work must be considered to ensure that dialysis treatments are not missed.

18.2.1 Hemodialysis

Patients undergoing facility-based hemodialysis may have multiple cardiovascular and diabetic comorbidities. In assessing their fitness to drive, physicians should evaluate these patients individually for the presence of relevant comorbidities, medications and adverse symptoms associated with their treatments.

Hemodialysis patients should not travel distances more than 1–2 days driving time from their home without making arrangements for dialysis at another centre. Even short trips may be prolonged by concurrent medical illness or inclement weather that closes roads or airports. Renal clinics have access to lists of dialysis centres both nationally and internationally that will accept traveling patients, and they can facilitate arrangements for dialysis abroad. The patient's overall health and stability on dialysis should be evaluated by his or her attending nephrologist before travel plans are initiated.

18.2.2 Peritoneal dialysis

Similar fitness-to-drive issues apply to peritoneal dialysis and hemodialysis patients. However, peritoneal dialysis is associated with slower, more continuous fluid removal, and thus symptoms relating to intravascular fluid shifts and hemodynamics are less of a problem.

18.3 Renal transplant

Drivers who have had a successful renal transplant and who have fully recovered from surgery can drive any class of motor vehicle.

Section 19
Musculoskeletal disabilities

Alert box

Immediate contraindications to driving*:
- inability to carry out visual checks by looking over the shoulder
- orthopedic braces (including neck)
- pain or marked reduction in range of motion resulting from an injury or impairment that may adversely affect driving ability
- pess than 4 weeks after total joint arthroplasty or less than 9 weeks after fixation displaced right ankle fracture.
- body or limb casts.

*A patient with any of these problems should be advised not to drive until the medical condition is evaluated and treated or resolved.

19.1　Overview

Musculoskeletal injury or disability can often have an impact on a patient's driving ability. In assessing a patient, keep in mind whether the patient drives a car with manual or automatic transmission.

All jurisdictions have established procedures to evaluate drivers whose medical condition is incompatible with medical standards, but who claim to be able to compensate and drive safely despite their condition. A driver in this situation, who is able to demonstrate that his or her driving remains safe, may be granted an exemption by the licensing agency. Periodic checks may be required by the licensing agency to validate the driver's maintenance of the ability to drive safely. A change in the medical condition of the driver may necessitate a new evaluation.

Patients with severe musculoskeletal impairment(s) should be considered for referral for complete functional assessment. They may be required to modify their vehicles with special controls.

19.2　Assessment

Musculoskeletal conditions differ in etiology and severity of physical impairment. However, all can have an impact on physical function, which may have a negative impact on driving. Few studies have investigated the relation between specific musculoskeletal conditions and the risk of motor vehicle crashes or their impact on driving ability. However, if there is any question that a physical impairment might affect the driver's ability to perform the required movements swiftly, accurately and repeatedly without undue pain, especially if the person plans to drive a passenger-carrying or commercial transport vehicle, the musculoskeletal system must be thoroughly and carefully assessed.

19.2.1   Fractures and casts

Physicians should be aware that any immobilization (even temporary) might have an impact on a driver's ability. Although any immobilization of a lower limb will have an obvious effect on the driver's operation of the pedals, especially in a vehicle with manual transmission, upper-limb immobilization can also detract from the operation of the hand controls, especially the steering wheel.

No one with an immobilized right leg should drive any vehicle. Immobilization of the left leg precludes driving a vehicle with manual transmission, as does immobilization of the right arm.

Immobilization of any limb or joint is incompatible with driving a motorcycle or scooter.

Driving should not be resumed until full function has returned to the immobilized limb. This can take some weeks after the removal of a cast.

19.2.2   Loss of limbs, deformities and prostheses

Those with a loss or deformity of the upper or lower extremities may drive any vehicle provided they can demonstrate their ability to drive to the satisfaction of the driver examiner. Many people with an amputation or deformity of one arm are able to drive a private vehicle safely. Some people with an amputation below the elbow who are fitted with an adequate prosthesis may operate any class of vehicle provided they demonstrate their ability to a driver examiner. People who have an amputation below the knee of one or both legs are usually able to drive any class of motor vehicle safely provided they have full strength and movement in their back, hips and knee joints and a properly fitted prosthesis or prostheses.

19.2.3   Arthritis

Degenerative or inflammatory arthritis can result in pain, loss of muscle strength, range of motion and function of the involved joint(s). People with arthritis may have difficulty turning their head to perform safety checks due to pain and stiffness of their cervical and thoracolumbar spine. Inflammatory arthritis can result in persistent pain and reduced range of movement in multiple joints including knees, ankles, hips, shoulders, elbows, wrists and hands. A patient should be restricted from driving if pain adversely affects their ability to drive safely or if he or she lacks range of movement or strength to execute the coordinated activities required. Most difficulties can be overcome by simple modifications to the vehicle or adjustment of driving technique. However, if there are concerns, the individual should be required to demonstrate his or her ability to a driver examiner.

19.2.4   *Spinal cord injuries*

Cervical: Some degree of loss of movement of the head and neck may be permitted, but the driver should then be restricted to driving vehicles equipped with panoramic mirrors, which may alleviate the need to do shoulder checks. People wearing a neck brace or cast or those with severe pain or very restricted range of movement should be advised not to drive until pain and restrictions of movement are minimal or appropriate adaptive devices are in place.

Thoracic: People with a marked deformity or painfully restricted motion in the thoracic vertebrae are not able to drive large commercial transport or passenger-carrying vehicles safely. Their ability to drive private vehicles can best be determined by a driver examiner. Patients wearing braces or body casts must be evaluated on the basis of their ability to move free of pain, operate the controls and observe approaching vehicles.

Lumbar: Applicants for a licence to drive a passenger transport or heavy commercial vehicle should be free of back pain that limits movement, attention or judgement. Less stringent standards may be applied to private-vehicle drivers. However, this group may need to be restricted to driving vehicles with power-assisted brakes.

19.2.5   *Post-orthopedic surgery*

Hip and knee arthroplasty: Movement precautions and activity restrictions following hip and knee arthroplasty are surgery and surgeon dependent. The ability to operate a vehicle safely is multifactorial, and brake response time is a key factor. Based on brake reaction time, 4-6 weeks is the recommended postoperative period to allow patients to resume driving, although input from the surgeon is critical due to other factors that may affect the individual's ability to resume driving.

Anterior cruciate ligament (ACL): Brake response times in rehabilitated patients following right ACL reconstruction are comparable to matched controls at 6 weeks after surgery. However, other factors such as pain and reduced range of motion may preclude them from driving safely. Therefore, discussion with the patient's surgeon is advisable before advising him or her that it is safe to resume driving.

Fixation of displaced ankle fracture: For patients with a fixation of a displaced right ankle fracture, normal braking function returns by 9 weeks. However, the decision to resume driving requires an assessment by the treating surgeon for other factors that may affect driving safety.

Paraplegia and quadriplegia: On the basis of a favourable recommendation from a medical specialist in physical medicine and rehabilitation, patients with new paraplegia or quadriplegia (below C4) may receive a learner's licence. With the permit, these patients may then take driving lessons in an adapted vehicle fitted with special, modified controls.

Section 20
General debility

20.1 Overview

"General debility" is defined as the sequelae of multiple medical conditions and syndromes that produce the specific and general symptoms of pain, fatigue, cachexia and physical disability, as well as cognitive symptoms of attention, concentration, memory and developmental and/or learning deficits. Medications used to combat the actual disease process as well as its signs and symptoms may produce effects that constitute part of the "general debility" state as well (see section 6, Drugs). With the expansion of medical knowledge and of medication therapies, this category becomes wider and its relevance to the issue of safety in driving becomes more important.

20.2 Common conditions

In addition to the general dictum that any medical condition can affect a person's ability to drive, the following specific conditions should be considered:
- anorexia nervosa or other related eating disorders
- chronic fatigue syndrome
- malabsorption syndromes
- chronic degenerative musculoskeletal syndromes (e.g., rheumatoid arthritis and other seronegative arthritides)
- AIDS
- malignancies
- congenital or acquired muscle diseases
- chronic painful conditions.

  The fitness to drive of patients with such conditions needs to be assessed on an individual basis. Further functional assessment is recommended (see section 2, Functional assessment — emerging emphasis).

Section 21
Anesthesia and surgery

Alert box
Any advice to the patient with respect to driving should be noted in the medical record.

21.1 Overview
Both anesthesia and surgery can have a significant, although temporary, effect on driving ability.

21.2 Outpatient surgery
Patients having outpatient surgery under general anesthesia should not drive for at least 24 hours. The pain and discomfort following even minor surgical procedures may extend this prohibition period several days.

21.3 Procedures
Any outpatient surgical or diagnostic procedure may render patients temporarily unfit to drive. Instructions to patients should include the necessity to provide a means to return home and the advisability of avoiding driving until all the effects of the procedure have resolved. Patients who do not have a means to return home should not undergo the planned procedure until arrangements have been made.

21.4 Major surgery
After major surgery, it is necessary to evaluate recovery individually. Any lingering or permanent effects of anesthesia should be subject to functional evaluation.

21.5 Conscious sedation
Anyone undergoing conscious sedation should be counseled to avoid driving for 24 hours.

Section 22
Seat belts and air bags

Alert box

There are no medical circumstances that justify exemption from wearing a seat belt.

22.1 Overview

All provinces and territories have legislation that require all occupants of a vehicle to wear seat belts. All children (including infants) must be secured in appropriate child seats.

If air bags are present in a vehicle, infants and children age 12 and under should sit only in the back seat of the vehicle. Air bags are safety devices that supplement the protection provided by seat belts. They are installed in the steering wheel and front passenger console of most newer model cars. There are still vehicles without them. In cars without air bags, the back seat is still safest in the event of a crash, as it is likely to be furthest from the point of impact.

A consumer can choose to have the air bag(s) in a vehicle deactivated if the consumer, or a user of the vehicle, is in one of the circumstances listed in section 22.3. An application form for deactivation of air bag(s) is available from Transport Canada. Physician documentation of the circumstance is not required. (See How to obtain a "Declaration of Requirement for Air Bag Deactivation" Form at www.tc.gc.ca/roadsafety/tp/tp13178/form_e.htm). People must indicate on the form that they have read the air bag deactivation brochure and understand the benefits and risks of deactivating the air bag.

22.2 Seat belts

Some provincial legislation allows for medical exemptions. However, there are no medical circumstances that justify exemption from wearing a seat belt.

Drivers who are uncomfortable wearing a seat belt should be encouraged to use devices such as belt extenders, adjustable seats, adjustable seat belts and padding to make the seat belt more comfortable.

Correct positioning of the seat belts, techniques such as the "pregnant woman technique" and coaching by occupational therapists and other interveners may facilitate the wearing of seat belts. Medical and paramedical personnel should consider seat belt pressure points when implanting invasive medical devices (e.g., medication pumps, cardiac pacemakers, vagal nerve stimulators, and intravenous entries).

22.3   Air bags

The one fact that is common to those seriously injured as a result of an air bag is NOT their height, weight, sex or age. It is the fact that they were too close to the air bag when it started to deploy. Infants and children age 12 years and under are vulnerable to serious injury by an air bag. Hence, children should be placed in the back seat.

Deactivating an air bag(s) may be reasonable in the following circumstances:

Drivers: A safe sitting distance (25 cm between sternum and the steering wheel) or position cannot be maintained because of scoliosis, achondroplasia, short legs or an unusual medical condition due to which the physician has informed the person that air bags pose a special risk to him or her.

Passengers:

- A safe sitting distance (25 cm between sternum and console) or position cannot be maintained because of scoliosis, Down's syndrome with atlantoaxial instability or an unusual medical condition, due to which the physician has informed the person that air bags pose a special risk to them or
- A passenger is an infant or child with a medical condition that requires him or her ride in the front seat for monitoring or
- A passenger is an infant or child and the vehicle does not have back seats.

For further information, contact:
Road Safety Information Centre
Transport Canada
Telephone: 800 333-0371
www.tc.gc.ca/roadsafety

Section 23
Motorcycles and off-road vehicles

23.1 Overview

Operating a motorcycle (Class 6) or an off-road vehicle, including a snowmobile, demands a higher level of physical fitness and different driving skills than driving a private passenger vehicle.

As long as off-road vehicles are not driven on provincial roads, they do not need licence plates, and their use is not subject to any regulation.

Nevertheless, drivers of motorcycles and off-road vehicles should be advised to wear protective helmets at all times. There are no valid medical reasons for a driver or a passenger not to wear a helmet. A person who is incapable of wearing a helmet should be encouraged to find another mode of transportation.

23.2 General

Motorcycle operators should be expected to meet the medical standards for private vehicle (Class 5) drivers in every respect. In doubtful cases, there is less room for compromise. Medical disabilities that might be overlooked for a private vehicle driver may be incompatible with the safe operation of a motorcycle.

Driving a motorcycle requires the full use of all four limbs and good balance. A motorcycle driver must be able to maintain a strong grip with both hands, as this is required for the use of handlebar controls. A driver must keep both hands on the handlebars.

23.3 Specific

Angina: Exposure to cold and cold winds can trigger an angina attack in susceptible patients.

Carotid sinus sensitivity: This condition is very dangerous because of tight restraining straps on most protective headgear, which may place pressure on the carotid sinus.

Cervical spine: Motorcycle drivers with a history of cervical spine injuries or instability should be assessed for the ability to maintain a safe riding posture without neurologic compromise.

Permanent tracheostomy: Drivers with a permanent tracheostomy should have some form of protection from the effects of the air stream.

Section 24
Aviation*

Alert box

Physicians are required by law to report to regional aviation medical officers of Transport Canada any pilots, air traffic controllers or flight engineers with a medical condition that could affect flight safety. Common conditions requiring mandatory reporting are listed in this section.

24.1   Overview

Note: For the purpose of this guide, all references to "pilots" will apply equally to air traffic controllers and flight engineers, unless otherwise stated. As well, "pilots" includes airline transport pilots, commercial pilots, private pilots, student pilots, recreational pilots, etc. The types of aircraft they may fly include fixed-wing planes (jet and propellor-driven), helicopters, balloons, gliders, ultra-lights and gyroplanes.

Pilots are all holders of Canadian aviation documents that impose standards of medical fitness. Regulation of pilots is under federal legislation (*not* provincial, as is the case for motor vehicle drivers).

Periodic examinations of pilots are performed by physicians (civil aviation medical examiners) appointed by the minister of transport. Episodic care of pilots is often by community physicians.

Before being examined, all pilots must inform the physician that they hold an aviation licence or permit. When pilots are informed that they have a condition (or are prescribed treatment) that might make it unsafe for them to perform their duties, they must "ground" themselves temporarily.

A physician diagnosing a condition that might affect flight safety must report the condition to the medical advisors of Transport Canada.

---

*Prepared by Transport Canada

24.2   *Aeronautics Act*

Section 6.5 of the *Aeronautics Act* describes the responsibilities of physicians with regard to pilots as follows:

1. Where a physician or an optometrist believes on reasonable grounds that a patient is a flight crew member, an air traffic controller or other holder of a Canadian aviation document that imposes standards of medical or optometric fitness, the physician or optometrist shall, if in his or her opinion the patient has a medical or optometric condition that is likely to constitute a hazard to aviation safety, inform a medical adviser designated by the Minister forthwith of that opinion and the reasons therefor.

2. The holder of a Canadian aviation document that imposes standards of medical or optometric fitness shall, prior to any medical or optometric examination of his/her person by a physician or optometrist, advise the physician or optometrist that he/she is the holder of such a document.

3. The Minister may make such use of any information provided pursuant to subsection (1) as he considers necessary in the interests of aviation safety.

4. No legal, disciplinary or other proceedings lie against a physician or optometrist for anything done by him in good faith in compliance with this section.

5. Notwithstanding subsection (3), information provided pursuant to subsection (1) is privileged and no person shall be required to disclose it or give evidence relating to it in any legal, disciplinary or other proceedings and the information so provided shall not be used in any such proceedings.

6. The holder of a Canadian aviation document that imposes standards of medical or optometric fitness shall be deemed, for the purposes of this section, to have consented to the giving of information to a medical adviser designated by the Minister under subsection (1) in the circumstances referred to in that subsection.

24.3   Reporting

If *uncertain* whether a condition might affect flight safety, the physician can discuss the case with a regional aviation medical officer (RAMO), as listed in section 24.20. At this stage, the physician need not identify the pilot.

If *certain* that a condition might affect flight safety, the physician must

*   Advise the pilot.
*   Report by phone to a RAMO at a civil aviation medicine regional office (see section 24.20). The report will be confidential, physician-to-physician and privileged.
*   Confirm information in writing (by facsimile). This report is confidential and privileged.

    Once a report under section 6.5 of the *Aeronautics Act* has been made, it is the RAMO's responsibility to take further action. Although Transport Canada may use the reported information as necessary to ensure aviation safety, the report itself cannot be used as evidence in any legal, disciplinary or other proceedings.

24.4   Medical conditions

This section is not intended to replace a textbook on aviation medicine. It is simply to alert community physicians to aspects of medical fitness that are of unique importance to aircrew and lists common reportable conditions.

Any condition or treatment that, in the treating physician's opinion, may interfere with flight safety, but is not found in this listing, should still be reported. If uncertain, the treating physician can contact their RAMO for guidance (see section 24.3, Reporting).

Further information on specific medical conditions may be obtained from the Civil Aviation Medicine branch of Transport Canada (www.tc.gc.ca/CivilAviation/Cam/).

24.5   General conditions

24.5.1   Hypoxia

Any condition that leads to a decrease in the supply of oxygen, its carriage in the blood or delivery to the tissues may worsen with increased altitude. Although individual tolerance varies, smoking, lung conditions, cardiac disease, anemia, alcohol and some drugs can increase the effects of hypoxia.

24.5.2   Gas expansion

Expansion of gas trapped in body cavities, such as the sinuses, the middle ear or the bowel, can be extremely uncomfortable and distracting. At high altitude, a small pneumothorax may be disabling.

24.5.3   Decompression illness

The recent use of compressed air in scuba diving can give rise to symptoms of decompression sickness even at the cabin altitudes common to pressurized aircraft.

24.5.4   Tolerance to increased acceleration

Pilots may be exposed to brief episodes of increased acceleration while in turbulence or during rapid manoeuvres to recover from unusual flight conditions. There is considerable individual variation in tolerance, but poor physical conditioning, illness, low blood pressure or the effects of medication may all lower the threshold for momentary loss of vision or loss of consciousness with increased acceleration stress.

24.5.5   *Spatial disorientation*

In flight, spatial orientation is maintained mainly by vision and vestibular balance organs. Any medical condition affecting balance organs or vision may induce or exaggerate dangerous spatial disorientation.

24.6   Vision

Conditions where visual impairment is temporary or vision is temporarily affected by the use of medications need not be reported. Pilots should be warned not to fly until normal vision has returned.

Reporting the following conditions is mandatory:

- diplopia
- monocularity
- visual fields — including partial loss of a visual field or significant scotomata
- eye injuries or retinal detachment
- cataract surgery
- surgical correction of myopia following radial keratotomy, photorefractive keratectomy, laser-assisted in-situ keratomileusis or other refractive eye surgery.

24.7   Ear, nose and throat

Significant deterioration in hearing must be reported. For the pilot, a normally functioning vestibular system is of the utmost importance, and any condition affecting balance or spatial orientation must be reported.

Reporting the following conditions is mandatory:

- hearing — sudden loss of hearing or conditions significantly affecting hearing
- middle-ear conditions — damage to the tympanic membranes or the eustachian tubes
- inner-ear conditions — any condition affecting or impinging on the inner ear or the vestibular (balance) organs
- stapedectomy and other ear surgery
- surgery affecting the nasal passages, sinuses or eustachian tubes
- conditions leading to voice distortion or inaudibility.

24.8   Cardiovascular conditions

The appearance of cardiovascular signs or symptoms is of great concern and must be discussed with the RAMO.

Detailed information on the assessment of particular cardiovascular conditions is available in the *Handbook for Civil Aviation Medical Examiners — Cardiovascular* (available online at www.tc.gc.ca/CivilAviation/Cam/TP13312-2/cardiovascular/menu.htm).

Reporting the following conditions is mandatory:
- cardiac inflammation and infection
- acute ischemic syndromes
  - angina pectoris — chest pain typical or atypical of angina pectoris
  - myocardial infarction
  - revascularization surgery or angioplasty (including stent insertion)
- cardiomyopathy
- cardiac transplantation.

24.8.1   Blood pressure

Medications with side effects of postural hypotension, arrhythmias or effects on the central nervous system are unacceptable.

Reporting the following conditions is mandatory:
- initial treatment of hypertension with medication
- symptomatic hypotension.

24.8.2   Valvular heart disease

Reporting the following conditions is mandatory:
- presence of significant heart disease
- development of new heart murmurs
- requirement for treatment
- repair or replacement of heart valves with prosthetic appliances.

Note: In view of the risk of thromboembolism, associated cardiac dysfunction, valve failure and bleeding secondary to anticoagulation, prosthetic valvular replacement candidates must be assessed individually by Civil Aviation Medicine.

24.8.3   Congenital heart disease (CHD)

Reporting the following conditions is mandatory:
- new diagnosis of CHD
- development of symptoms in a pilot with known CHD.

24.8.4   Cardiac arrhythmia

Even benign arrhythmias can cause distraction, which, during critical phases of flight, may cause an incident or accident. A physician evaluating any pilot with an arrhythmia should bear the following points in mind: How disabled is the pilot when the arrhythmia occurs? Is there structural heart disease present? Serious consideration should be given to reporting any arrhythmia.

Reporting the following conditions is mandatory:

- premature atrial or ventricular contraction — when these are symptomatic or require medication for control
- paroxysmal tachyarrhythmias — all tachyarrhythmias, even if they appear to be asymptomatic
- atrial fibrillation and flutter — at their onset and when any change in treatment is required
- sinus node dysfunction or sick sinus syndrome — symptomatic bradycardia or sinus node dysfunction
- heart block and bundle branch blocks — second- or third-degree heart block or the development of a new right or left bundle branch block
- pacemakers — pilots requiring a pacemaker or automatic implantable defibrillation devices.

24.9   Cerebrovascular disorders

Pilots who show any evidence of memory loss, poor concentration or diminished alertness must be reported.

Reporting of the following is mandatory:

- transient ischemic attacks (TIA) or cerebral artery stenosis that has led to confusion, disturbance of vision, attacks of vertigo or loss of consciousness
- stroke — completed stroke or any other cerebrovascular accident
- carotid endarterectomy
- asymptomatic carotid bruits — where investigation indicates significant carotid obstruction (more than 50%).

24.10   Other vascular disorders

Superficial thrombophlebitis without complications need *not* be reported.

Reporting of the following is mandatory:

- aortic aneurysms
- symptomatic or enlarging thoracic aneurysm or abdominal aneurysm 5 cm in diameter or greater
- recent surgical repair of an aneurysm
- deep venous thrombosis.

24.11   Nervous system

Disorders of the central nervous system can be a potent source of occult incapacitation. Lapses of consciousness or memory in the aviation environment can be fatal.

Detailed information on assessment of particular neurological conditions is available in the *Handbook for Civil Aviation Medical Examiners — Neurology* (available online at www.tc.gc.ca/CivilAviation/Cam/tp13312-2/neurology/menu.htm).

Reporting of the following is mandatory:

- syncope — unexplained loss of consciousness, whatever the cause
- seizure disorders
- head injuries — any significant head injury, particularly if it is associated with unconsciousness or post-traumatic amnesia
- sleep disorders of any type
- vestibular disorders — spatial disorientation is a significant cause of aviation accidents and is a contributing cause in 30% of fatal accidents. Any condition that interferes even temporarily with balance or coordination must be reported
- headache — migraine with aura; may include visual loss, cognitive impairment and other neurological deficits. Any type of severe or prolonged headache requiring medications that may produce unacceptable side effects
- disorders of coordination and muscular control — any condition affecting coordination and muscular control.

24.12 Respiratory diseases

Gradual deterioration of the respiratory system over years may not be obvious, particularly if the pilot does not complain or is using bronchodilator medications. Physicians treating pilots must remain alert to the risk of hypoxia and trapped gas expansion (e.g., pneumothorax) when deciding on treatment.

Reporting of the following is mandatory:

- chronic obstructive pulmonary disease — significant decreases in pulmonary function, decreased arterial oxygen saturation, increasing hypercapnia or recurrent infections
- asthma — increasing requirement for inhaled bronchodilators or steroids; use of medications containing aminophylline
- pneumothorax — spontaneous pneumothorax, pleural blebs, lung cysts or other conditions that may lead to problems with trapped gas expansion (this may be of less significance in air traffic controllers)
- pulmonary embolism
- sarcoidosis.

24.13 Endocrine and metabolic disorders

Detailed information on particular diabetic conditions is available in the *Handbook for Civil Aviation Medical Examiners — Diabetes* (available online at www.tc.gc.ca/CivilAviation/Cam /tp13312-2/diabetes/menu.htm).

Reporting of the following is mandatory:

- diabetes mellitus
  - Type 1 diabetes (insulin-dependent) — when first diagnosed. Pilots and air traffic controllers requiring insulin are considered on an individual basis.
  - Type 2 diabetes (non-insulin-dependent) — at first requirement for antihyperglycemic drugs; changes in type or dose of medication; hypoglycemic attacks requiring treatment
- thyroid and parathyroid disease — Initial diagnosis of these conditions. Once the condition is stable, only significant changes in treatment.
- pituitary disease — Initial diagnosis and investigation
- adrenal disease — Initial diagnosis and investigation
- anabolic steroids.

24.14   Renal system

Reporting of the following is mandatory:

- renal colic or the discovery of kidney or bladder stones
- developing renal failure or undergoing renal dialysis
- requirement for renal transplantation. After successful transplantation, only significant changes in treatment.

24.15   Musculoskeletal system

Reporting of the following is mandatory:

- recent amputation of a limb or part of a limb
- arthritis — symptomatic patients whose mobility becomes restricted; those with side effects from required medications (e.g., nonsteroidal anti-inflammatory drugs); those requiring second- or third-stage medications (e.g., gold, azathioprine).

24.16   Psychiatric disorders

In an occupation as potentially hazardous as flying, the level of tolerance for psychiatric disorders or disease is small. Even when symptoms are effectively treated, the side effects of psychoactive drugs, such as selective serotonin reuptake inhibitors (SSRIs), are usually unacceptable.

Pilots with emotional disorders may be reluctant to discuss their condition with a civil aviation medical examiner and will more likely seek advice and treatment from a community physician. Physicians are strongly urged to discuss such cases with the RAMO.

Reporting of the following is mandatory:

- cognitive disorders — dementia, as soon as suspected or diagnosed
- psychosis — this includes bipolar affective disorder

- emotional disorders — these conditions may be temporary and stress induced; when they require drug therapy or may interfere with judgement, decision-making or reaction time, they must be reported

24.17   Tumours
Reporting of the following is mandatory:
- any tumour that limits the ability of a pilot to perform safely
- tumours that may metastasize to the brain.

24.18   HIV infection and AIDS
Reporting of the following is mandatory:
- positive test for HIV
- diagnosis of AIDS.

24.19   Drugs
- *Substance abuse:* Pilots who abuse or are addicted to alcohol or other chemical substances must be reported.
- *Alcohol:* By law, no one may function as a crew member of an aircraft (or work as an ATC) if he or she has consumed alcohol within the previous 8 hours. After heavy drinking, even this interval will be too short because alcohol can affect balance and orientation for up to 48 hours.
- *Illicit drugs:* Marijuana and other illicit drugs impair judgement and coordination; the effects may last for prolonged periods.
- *Prescription drugs:* Discuss in detail the side effects of any medication that is prescribed or recommended to pilots. For example, minor side effects on visual accommodation, muscular coordination, the gastrointestinal tract or tolerance to acceleration (increased gravity) may be more serious when they occur in flight. If in doubt, the physician should discuss the medication with the RAMO.
- *Over-the-counter drugs:* Generally, pilots are advised to avoid taking any medication within 12 hours (or, if longer-acting, within about 5 half-lives) before flight if pharmacologic effects may affect flying. Although there are exceptions to this rule, caution is advised.
- *Anesthetics (general and local):* There is no general rule about how long a pilot should be grounded after receiving a general anesthetic. It depends on the type of surgery, pre-medication and the anesthetic agent. Physicians should be aware that the effect of some anesthetics may take days to wear off, and caution is recommended. A RAMO can answer enquiries on this subject.

In cases where local anesthetics have been used for extensive procedures, flying should be restricted for a minimum of 24 hours.

24.20   Contacts

Civil Aviation Medicine headquarters
Civil Aviation Medicine
Transport Canada
330 Sparks St.
Place de Ville, Tower C, Room 617
Ottawa ON K1A 0N8
Telephone: 613 990-1311
Toll free: 888 764-3333
Fax: 613 990-6623
www.tc.gc.ca/CivilAviation/Cam/

Civil Aviation Medicine Branch offices (Regional aviation medical officers)
Atlantic region (New Brunswick, Nova Scotia, PEI, Newfoundland and Labrador)
Ottawa, Ontario
Telephone: 888 764-3333; 613 990-4247; Fax: 613 990-6623

Quebec
Dorval, Québec
Telephone: 888 570-5712; 514 633-3258; Fax: 514 633-3247

Ontario
North York, Ontario
Telephone: 877 726-8694; 416 952-0562; Fax: 416 952-0569

Prairie and northern region (Alberta, Yukon, Manitoba, Saskatchewan, Northwest
Territories and Nunavut)
Edmonton AB
Telephone: 877 855-4643; 780 495-3848; Fax: 780 495-4905

Pacific region (British Columbia)
Vancouver, BC
Telephone: 877 822-2229; 604 666-5601; Fax: 604 666-0145

Section 25
Railway*

25.1   Overview

This section concerns assessing medical fitness for duty of a person occupying a safety critical position on a railway. These employees operate or control the movement of trains. As a general rule, they are required, at a minimum, to meet the medical standards expected of a commercial driver (i.e., Class 1 licence).

Assessments regarding fitness for duty, as well as episodic medical care, are usually done by community physicians.

A person in a safety critical position must identify themselves as such to a physician before any examination.

The occupations designated as safety critical positions may vary between railways, but typically include
- locomotive engineer
- conductor
- assistant conductor (brakeperson)
- yard foreman or yardperson
- rail traffic controller (train dispatcher).

---

*Prepared by the Medical Advisory Group of the Railway Association of Canada to facilitate public safety in rail freight and passenger train operations across Canada.

In addition, any employee or contractor who is required to perform any of these functions is considered to occupy a safety critical position.

25.2   Railway Safety Act

The *Railway Safety Act* (RSA) is federal legislation that gives the minister of transport jurisdiction over railway safety matters. It is regulated by Transport Canada and covers railway safety, security and the environment. Section 35 of the RSA mandates regular medical examinations for all persons occupying safety critical positions. The RSA

- requires that physicians and optometrists notify the railway company's chief medical officer if a person occupying a safety critical position has a medical condition that could be a threat to safe railway operations and that the physician or optometrist send a copy of this notice without delay to the patient
- makes it the responsibility of the patient to inform the physician or optometrist that he or she holds a designated safety critical position at the time of any examination
- allows the railway company to use the information provided by the physician or optometrist in the interests of safe railway operations
- prohibits any legal, disciplinary or other proceedings against a physician or optometrist for such information given in good faith
- prohibits further disclosure, or use as evidence, of such medical information, except with the permission of the patient.

25.3   Reporting

According to the *Railway Safety Act*, a physician must notify a railway company's chief medical officer if a person occupying a safety critical position has a medical condition that could be a threat to safe railway operations. Contact information is listed in section 25.8.

25.4   Medical fitness

Railway medical rules for safety critical positions have been developed by the Medical Steering Committee of the Railway Association of Canada and approved by the minister of transport. These rules set out requirements for frequency of medical assessments and also allow for individual assessment of medical fitness for duty.

The chief medical officer of each railway company may increase the frequency of medical assessments, restrict a person from occupying a safety critical position, apply restrictions on the performance of certain tasks or require the use of corrective devices or other medical aids.

25.5   General considerations

Capabilities that must be reviewed when considering medical fitness for duty of any person

in a railway safety critical position include, but are not limited to
- Cognition. The person must have normal function in terms of
  - alertness
  - judgement
  - concentration
  - comprehension of *concurrent* written, verbal and signal-based communication
  - awareness of the environment and other members of the work crew and
  - vigilance for prolonged periods.
- Special senses
  - Vision, including colour perception, must meet railway industry standards. Individuals not meeting colour vision testing standards are required to undergo further assessment by a specific test developed by the railway industry.
  - Hearing must meet railway industry standards. Despite noisy environments, railway workers must be able to receive, comprehend, and transmit communications via a variety of means (e.g., radio, telephone, face to face).
  - Ability to tolerate and function in a stressful work environment, which includes a highly variable work shift.
  - Must not be subject to sudden impairment of physical or mental capabilities.

Medical fitness for duty also takes into consideration medical conditions including treatment and medications, both past and present, that could result in
- sudden or gradual impairment of cognitive function including alertness, judgement, insight, memory and concentration
- impairment of senses
- significant impairment of musculoskeletal function
- other impairment that is likely to constitute a threat to safe railway operations.

Note: Railway medical guidelines (see section 25.7) include the following conditions to assist physicians regarding safety critical positions:
- cardiovascular disorders
- diabetes
- epilepsy or other epileptic seizures
- hearing
- mental disorders
- severe sleep apnea
- substance use disorders
- vision.

Medical conditions not currently covered by a specific guideline are governed by accepted medical practice.

25.6   Specific issues

Medical fitness requirements must also be assessed for specific capabilities associated with the following safety critical positions:

Locomotive engineer

- Must be able to walk, climb and very occasionally lift 36 kg (80 lb) from floor to waist level.
- May have to walk extended distances in variable weather conditions and on uneven terrain.

Conductor, brakeperson, yardperson

- Must be able to walk, climb and occasionally lift 36 kg (80 lb) from floor to waist level.
- Must be able to walk in variable weather conditions and on uneven terrain.
- Good strength and endurance is required in the arms, shoulders and upper back. For example, performing track switching duties requires
  - 17–19 kg (37–41 lb) of force to lift switch lever
  - 18–27 kg (40–60 lb) of force to pull switch over
  - 17–19 kg (37–41 lb) of force to lock switch lever back in place.
- A good sense of balance is required as these tasks are performed outdoors where terrain may be uneven and slippery, wet, icy or snow covered.

Railway traffic controller (RTC)

- Must be able to sit for prolonged periods. Limited physical demands.
- Must have the ability to use a keyboard to enter instructions.
- Must be able to concentrate for prolonged periods while viewing a computer screen and listening and reacting to communications simultaneously.

25.7   Resources

A copy of the *Canadian Railway Medical Rules Handbook* (which includes the current *Railway Medical Guidelines*) is available on Railway Association of Canada Web site: www.railcan.ca/documents/circulars/657/2004_11_01_CMR_Handbook_en.pdf

25.8   Contacts

Canadian Pacific Railway
Occupational Health Services
Telephone: 866 876-0879 (toll free)

CN
Occupational Health Services
Telephone: 514 399-5690

VIA Rail Canada
Telephone: 800 363-6737

Railway Association of Canada
Office of the Vice-President
Operations and Regulatory Affairs
Telephone: 613 564-8088

Appendix A
Fitness to drive issues and risk management messages from the CMPA

In Canada most people are dependant on their vehicles for activities of daily living and many others for earning a living. A report from a physician resulting in the loss of the right to operate a vehicle provokes strong feelings and can have serious personal and financial consequences for the individuals involved. The thought of having an unfit driver endangering the lives of him/her self and others is equally abhorrent. As with many things in medicine, reporting or not reporting to the motor vehicle authorities patients with a medical condition that may render them unfit to drive requires careful consideration. The final decision can have implications, some of them serious, for both the physician and patient.

There is a statutory duty in all jurisdictions related to reporting a patient who may have a medical condition that may render him or her unfit to drive. The relevant legislation in some jurisdictions is discretionary such that physicians are permitted to breach confidence and report such patients. In other jurisdictions the legislation is mandatory and requires physicians to report any patient who, in their opinion, has a medical condition that may make it dangerous for the person to drive.

The Canadian Medical Protective Association recently reviewed its experience in assisting members in matters related to fitness to drive. In addition to scores of advice calls there have been 39 medico–legal cases concluded between 2001 and 2005 involving this topic. They have been evenly split between complaints to the regulatory authorities (college) and legal actions or threats of legal actions.

There are 3 principal themes in the cases. The first is the failure to report a patient's medical condition to the authorities. The second is complaints from the patient that a report had been made and the third is related to dissatisfaction that the physician would not agree to write to the authorities in support of the licence being reinstated.

Failure to report
Following a motor vehicle accident caused by an unfit driver the allegation can be that the accident would not have occurred but for the lack of appropriate reporting on the physician's part. Physicians have been found liable for damages under these circumstances.

The most frequent diagnosis involved in a failure to report is a seizure disorder. While the legislative requirements vary with each jurisdiction, there are some common features in the cases. Physicians need to be aware of the relevant legislative requirements in their jurisdiction. Each will have to comply with the legislation. Particularly where more than one physician is treating a patient there can be an assumption that one of the other physicians has made a report when in fact no report has been made. Uncertainty about what medical conditions require reporting can be an issue and this booklet will be an excellent guide. Appropriate consultations with specialists in the clinical area involved may also be helpful in some situations. The physical and mental requirements to operate a particular vehicle may also require assessment and testing.

The administrative process for the authorities to assess the reports and decide on a course of action takes time. Patients considered to have a medical condition that may render them unfit to drive should be warned not to drive until the authorities have made and communicated a final decision. This should be clearly documented on the clinical record.

Complaints about reporting

This is the largest category of cases. Patients learning that the authorities have restricted their driving privileges are understandably upset. This is particularly the case if the notification was the first they have heard about the matter. Remember, it is the physician who reports, but the decision about any restrictions is that of the authorities. Prior to making the report, it is very helpful to have a discussion with your patient about your intent to report to the authorities and the nature of your report.

Common clinical circumstances in the cases reviewed are diagnoses of seizure disorders, alcohol and drug abuse and psychiatric disorders.

Reinstatement

The final category of cases relates to complaints that physicians would not support a patient's request to have their licence reinstated. While temporary restrictions on operating a motor vehicle are tolerated by many patients, some find the longer-term consequences an increasing burden. Physicians are sometimes pressured to assist patients in regaining licensure. Careful consideration should be given to evaluating the clinical risks of the patient prior to any such report being sent.

Risk management

- Familiarize yourself and comply with the relevant legislation in your jurisdiction.
- Each treating physician must comply with the legislation when required.
- Obtain consultations with specialists as appropriate to assist with the assessment of the patient.

- Disability (functional) assessments (e.g., cognitive, musculoskeletal, vision, etc.) may be indicated.
- Limit the report to the information prescribed by the legislation.
- Inform the patient in advance of your intent to report.
- Document your assessment and the fact you have reported.
- Caution the patient not to drive (if appropriate) until the authorities make a final determination. Document your advice.
- Seizure disorders, alcohol and drug abuse and psychiatric diagnoses are high-risk diagnoses.
- Careful clinical reassessments should be done prior to considering supporting a request to reinstate a patient's licence.

Appendix B
CAGE questionnaire

- Have you ever felt you should **C**ut down on your drinking?
- Have people **A**nnoyed you by criticizing your drinking?
- Have you ever felt bad or **G**uilty about your drinking?
- Have you ever had a drink first thing in the morning to steady your nerves or to get rid of a hangover (**E**ye opener)?

Scoring

Item responses on the CAGE are scored 0 or 1, with a higher score an indication of alcohol problems. A total score of 2 or greater is considered clinically significant.

. . . .

Developed by Dr. John Ewing, founding director of the Bowles Center for Alcohol Studies, University of North Carolina at Chapel Hill, CAGE is an internationally used assessment instrument for identifying alcoholics. It is particularly popular with primary caregivers. CAGE has been translated into several languages.

The CAGE questions can be used in the clinical setting using informal phrasing. It has been demonstrated that they are most effective when used as part of a general health history and should NOT be preceded by questions about how much or how frequently the patient drinks (see DL Steinweg and H Worth. Alcoholism: the keys to the CAGE. *American Journal of Medicine* 1993;94:520-3).

The exact wording that can be used in research studies can be found in: JA Ewing Detecting alcoholism: the CAGE questionnaire. *JAMA* 1984;252:1905-7. Researchers and clinicians who are publishing studies using the CAGE questionnaire should cite the above reference. No other permission is necessary unless it is used in any profit-making endeavour, which would require negotiating payment.

Appendix C
Alcohol use disorders identification test (AUDIT)*

Read questions as written. Record answers carefully. Begin the AUDIT by saying, "Now I am going to ask you some questions about your use of alcoholic beverages during the past year." Explain what is meant by "alcoholic beverages" using local examples of beer, wine, vodka, etc. Code answers in terms of "standard drinks." Place the correct answer number in the box at the right.

1. How often do you have a drink containing alcohol?
Never	(0)
[Skip to questions 9 and 10]	
Monthly or less	(1)
2 to 4 times a month	(2)
2 to 3 times a week	(3)
4 or more times a week	(4)

2. How many drinks containing alcohol do you have on a typical day when you are drinking?
1 or 2	(1)
3 or 4	(2)
5 or 6	(3)
7, 8 or 9	(4)
10 or more	(5)

3. How often do you have six or more drinks on one occasion?
Never	(0)
Less than monthly	(1)
Monthly	(2)
Weekly	(3)
Daily or almost daily	(4)

    Skip to questions 9 and 10 if total score for questions 2 and 3 = 0

4. How often during the last year have you found that you were not able to stop drinking once you had started?
Never	(0)
Less than monthly	(1)
Monthly	(2)
Weekly	(3)
Daily or almost daily	(4)

5. How often during the last year have you failed to do what was normally expected from you because of drinking?
Never	(0)
Less than monthly	(1)
Monthly	(2)
Weekly	(3)
Daily or almost daily	(4)

*Babor TF, Higgins-Biddle JC, Sanders JB, Monteiro MG. AUDIT — alcohol use disorders identification test: guidelines for use in primary care. Geneva: World Health Organization. Geneva; 2001. WHO/MSD/MSB/01.6a. Reprinted with permission.

6. How often during the last year have you needed a first drink on awakening to get yourself going after a heavy drinking session?

Never	(0)
Less than monthly	(1)
Monthly	(2)
Weekly	(3)
Daily or almost daily	(4)

7. How often during the last year have you had a feeling of guilt or remorse after drinking?

Never	(0)
Less than monthly	(1)
Monthly	(2)
Weekly	(3)
Daily or almost daily	(4)

8. How often during the last year have you been unable to remember what happened the night before because you had been drinking?

Never	(0)
Less than monthly	(1)
Monthly	(2)
Weekly	(3)
Daily or almost daily	(4)

9. Have you or someone else been injured as the result of your drinking?

No	(0)
Yes, but not in the last year	(2)
Yes, during the last year	(4)

10. Has a relative or friend or a doctor or other health worker been concerned about your drinking or suggested you cut down?

No	(0)
Yes, but not in the last year	(2)
Yes, during the last year	(4)

Record total of items here _____

A score of 8 or greater may indicate the need for a more in-depth assessment.

Appendix D
Driving and dementia toolkit

The following information is from The Driving and Dementia Toolkit that was developed by members of the Dementia Network of Ottawa-Carleton and the Regional Geriatric Assessment Program — modified for purposes of this guide. The full document can be found at www.rgapottawa.com/dementia/default.asp (©2001 Regional Geriatric Assessment Program of Ottawa-Carleton).

Strategies

10 questions to ask the patient

	Yes	No
1. Have you noticed any change in your driving skills?	❏	❏
2. Do others honk at you or show signs of irritation?	❏	❏
3. Have you lost any confidence in your overall driving ability, leading you to drive less often or only in good weather?	❏	❏
4. Have you ever become lost while driving?	❏	❏
5. Have you ever forgotten where you were going?	❏	❏
6. Do you think that at present you are an unsafe driver?	❏	❏
7. Have you had any car accidents in the last year?	❏	❏
8. Any minor fender-benders with other cars in parking lots?	❏	❏
9. Have you received any traffic citations for speeding, going too slow, improper turns, failure to stop, etc.?	❏	❏
10. Have others criticized your driving or refused to drive with you?	❏	❏

10 questions to ask the family

	Yes	No
1. Do you feel uncomfortable in any way driving with the patient?	❏	❏
2. Have you noted any abnormal or unsafe driving behaviour?	❏	❏
3. Has the patient had any recent crashes?	❏	❏

	Yes	No
4. Has the patient had near-misses that could be attributed to mental or physical decline?	❏	❏
5. Has the patient received any tickets or traffic violations	❏	❏
6. Are other drivers forced to drive defensively to accommodate the patient's errors in judgement?	❏	❏
7. Have there been any occasions where the patient has gotten lost or experienced navigational confusion?	❏	❏
8. Does the person need many cues or directions from passengers?	❏	❏
9. Does the patient need a co-pilot to alert them of potentially hazardous events or conditions?	❏	❏
10. Have others commented on the patient's unsafe driving?	❏	❏

Cautionary note: In some cases the answers may not reflect the full picture as the family or patient may want to preserve the driving privilege.

What to tell your patients
Explain compensatory strategies, if appropriate
1. Drive only familiar routes
2. Drive slowly
3. Don't drive at night
4. Don't use the radio because it can be distracting
5. Avoid busy intersections
6. Don't drive with a distracting companion
7. Take a 55 Alive course (a classroom refresher course designed for seniors to improve and/or refresh their driving status)
8. Avoid expressways
9. Avoid rush hour traffic

How to tell the patient he or she is unsafe to drive
1. Discuss your concerns about driving with the patient and their caregivers. Be firm and non-negotiable in your instructions that they do not drive.
2. Provide a **written** statement to the patient of your reasons to challenge their fitness to drive and give a copy to the caregiver (see sample below).
3. Communicate in writing your legal obligation and intention to notify the ministry of transportation.

4. Explore transportation options and alternative ways of promoting autonomy for patient with progressive dementia.
5. Explore options such as Para Transpo, volunteer drivers or contracts with taxi companies.
6. Explain your concern for his/her safety and safety of others.
7. Some individuals may be more receptive to stopping driving based on concomitant medical disorders (such as impaired vision).
8. For non-compliant drivers, encourage family to confiscate keys, change locks, deactivate ignition or battery or park at a distant location. The caregiver may have to consider selling the car.
9. Avoid arguing with the person (who may have limited insight).
10. Spend your time and energy on helping to preserve the patient's dignity by focusing on the activities he or she can still do and enjoy.

Sample of written statement for the patient

Date

Name
Address

Dear Mr (Mrs):

It is my legal responsibility to notify the Ministry of Transportation if there is any concern regarding driving safety.

You have undergone assessment at
_____.

I am recommending that you do not drive for the following reasons:
_____
_____
_____
_____

Best regards,
_____, MD

Cognitive loss and driving: the resources algorithm for physicians

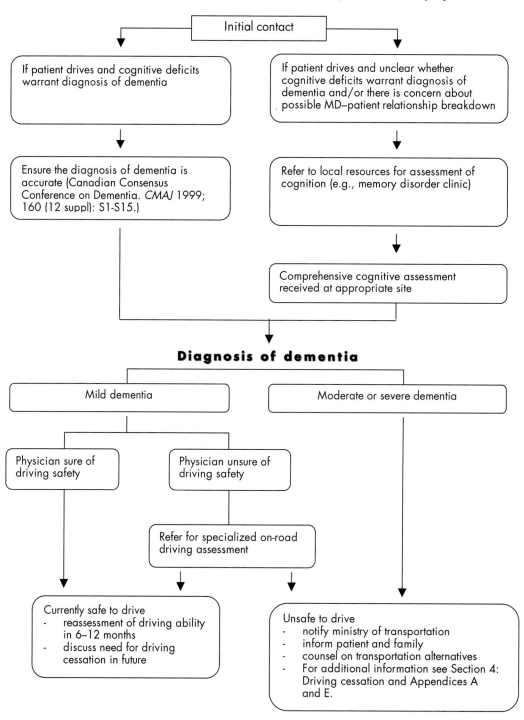

Initial contact

If patient drives and cognitive deficits warrant diagnosis of dementia

If patient drives and unclear whether cognitive deficits warrant diagnosis of dementia and/or there is concern about possible MD–patient relationship breakdown

Ensure the diagnosis of dementia is accurate (Canadian Consensus Conference on Dementia. *CMAJ* 1999; 160 (12 suppl): S1-S15.)

Refer to local resources for assessment of cognition (e.g., memory disorder clinic)

Comprehensive cognitive assessment received at appropriate site

Diagnosis of dementia

Mild dementia

Moderate or severe dementia

Physician sure of driving safety

Physician unsure of driving safety

Refer for specialized on-road driving assessment

Currently safe to drive
- reassessment of driving ability in 6–12 months
- discuss need for driving cessation in future

Unsafe to drive
- notify ministry of transportation
- inform patient and family
- counsel on transportation alternatives
- For additional information see Section 4: Driving cessation and Appendices A and E.

Appendix E
Provincial and territorial contact information for reporting potentially unfit drivers*

Driver assessment centres and rehabilitation resources can also be located in your area by contacting these offices.

ALBERTA
Director, Driver Fitness and Monitoring Branch
Infrastructure & Transportation
Main Floor Twin Atria Bldg
4999–98 Avenue
Edmonton AB T6B 2X3
Tel. : 780 427-8230
www3.gov.ab.ca/gs/services/mv

BRITISH COLUMBIA
Office of the Superintendent of Motor Vehicles
PO Box 9254, Stn Prov Gov
Victoria BC V8W 9J2
Tel.: 250 387-7747
Fax: 250 387-4891
osmv.mailbox@gov.bc.ca
www.pssg.gov.bc.ca/osmv/information/contact.htm

MANITOBA
Medical Records Section
Driver and Vehicle Licensing
Box 6300
1075 Portage Ave.
Winnipeg MB R3C 4A4
Tel.: Public 204 985-1900
or toll free 866 617-6676
Physicians 204 985-7381
Fax: 204 953-4992
www.mpi.mb.ca

NEW BRUNSWICK
Medical Advisory Board
Department of Public SafetyMotor Vehicle Branch
Box 6000
Fredericton NB E3B 5H1
Tel.: 506 453-2410
Fax: 506 453-7455
www.gnb.ca/0276/vehicle/index-e.asp

*As of August 2006.

NEWFOUNDLAND AND LABRADOR

Medical Review Officer
Dept. of Government Services and Lands
Motor Registration Division
Box 8710
St. John's NF A1B 4J5
Tel.: 709 729-0345
Fax: 709 729-4360
www.gs.gov.nl.ca

NORTHWEST TERRITORIES

Road Licensing & Safety Division
Department of Transportation Government of
the Northwest Territories
Box 1320
Yellowknife NT X1A 2L9
Tel.: 867 873-7406
Fax: 867 873-0120
www.gov.nt.ca/Transportation

NOVA SCOTIA

Service Nova Scotia & Municipal Relations
Road Safety Programs
1505 Barrington St., 9th floor
North Halifax NS B3J 3K5
Tel.: 902 424-5732
Fax: 902 424-0772
www.gov.ns.ca/snsmr/rmv/licence/medicals.asp

NUNAVUT

Kitikmeot Region, Head Quarters
Motor Vehicles Division
Community Government and Transportation
Government of Nunavut
PO Box 207
Gjoa Haven NU X0B 1J0
Tel.: 867 360-4616
Fax: 867 360-4619
www.gov.nu.ca

ONTARIO

Registrar of Motor Vehicles
Medical Review Section
Ministry of Transportation
2680 Keele St.
Downsview ON M3M 3E6
Tel.: 416 235-1773 or Toll free 800 268-1481
Fax: 416 235-3400 or 800 304-7889
www.mto.gov.on.ca/english/dandv/driver
/medreport/index

PRINCE EDWARD ISLAND

Registrar, Highway Safety
Box 2000
Charlottetown PE C1A 7N8
Tel.: 902 368-5210
Fax: 902 368-5236
www.gov.pe.ca/infopei/index.php3?number=889

QUÉBEC

Service de l'évaluation médicale
Société de l'assurance automobile du Québec
333, boul. Jean-Lesage, N-4-34
CP 19600
Québec QC G1K 8J6
Tel.: 418 643-5506; outside Québec 800 561-
2858
Fax: 418 643-4840
www.saaq.gouv.qc.ca

SASKATCHEWAN

Saskatchewan Government Insurance
Medical Review Unit
2260–11th Avenue, 3rd floor
Regina SK S4P 2N7
Tel.: 306 775-6176 or toll free 800 667-8015
x6176
Fax: 306 347-2577 or 866 274-4417
mruinquiries@sgi.sk.ca
www.sgi.sk.ca

YUKON

Sanctions Officer
Government of Yukon
Ministry of Community Services C-22
Box 2703
Whitehorse YT Y1A 2C6
Tel.: 867 667-3563
Fax: 867 393-6220
www.community.gov.yk.ca

Appendix F
Canadian Cardiovascular Society's risk of harm formula*

The risk of harm (RH) to other road users posed by the driver with heart disease is assumed to be directly proportional to the following:
- time spent behind the wheel or distance driven in a given time period (TD)
- type of vehicle driven (V)
- risk of sudden cardiac incapacitation (SCI)
- the probability that such an event will result in a fatal or injury-producing accident (Ac).

Expressing this statement as Formula 1:

$$RH = TD \times V \times SCI \times Ac$$

Fewer than 2% of reported incidents of driver sudden death or loss of consciousness have resulted in injury or death to other road users or bystanders.[1–4] In Formula 1, therefore, Ac = 0.02 for all drivers.

There is evidence that loss of control of a heavy truck or passenger-carrying vehicle results in a more devastating accident than loss of control of a private automobile[5]. Truckers are involved in only about 2% of all road accidents but in approximately 7.2% of all fatal accidents.[5] In Formula 1, if V = 1 for a commercial driver, then V = 0.28 for a private driver.

There is no published standard or definition of what level of risk is considered acceptable in Canada even through this is crucial in the formulation of guidelines based on the probability of some event occurring in a defined time period. It was necessary, therefore, to develop such a standard.

For several years, the guidelines of the Canadian Cardiovascular Society, the Canadian Medical Association, and the Canadian Council of Motor Transport Administrators have permitted the driver of a heavy truck to return to that occupation following an acute myocardial infarction provided that he or she is functional class I with a negative exercise stress test at 7 metabolic equivalents, has no disqualifying ventricular arrhythmias and is at least 3 months post-infarct. On the basis of available data, however, such a person cannot be assigned a risk lower than 1% of cardiac death in the next year. The risk of sudden death

*Excerpt from the Canadian Cardiovascular Society Consensus Conference 2003: *Assessment of the cardiac patient for fitness to drive and fly* (final report). Adapted with permission from the *Canadian Journal of Cardiology*.

would be lower than this, but would be at least partly offset by the risk of other suddenly disabling events such as syncope or stroke. For such a person, SCI is estimated to be equal to 0.01 in Formula 1.

It may be assumed that the average commercial driver spends 25% of his or her time behind the wheel.[5] Thus, in Formula 1, TD = 0.25. As indicated above, V may be assigned a value of 1 for commercial drivers and Ac = 0.02 for all drivers. Substituting into Formula 1:

$$RH = TD \times V \times SCI \times Ac$$
$$= 0.25 \times 1 \times 0.01 \times 0.02$$
$$= 0.00005$$

Allowing such a driver on the road is associated with an annual risk of death or injury to others of approximately 1 in 20 000 (0.00005). This level of risk appears to be generally acceptable in Canada.

A similar standard may be applied to the driver of a private automobile. The average private driver spends approximately 4% of his or her time behind the wheel (TD = 0.04).[6] As indicated above, for such a driver, V = 0.28 and Ac = 0.02. The acceptable yearly risk of sudden death or cardiac incapacitation for such a person would be calculated as follows:

$$RH = TD \times V \times SCI \times Ac$$
$$0.00005 = 0.04 \times 0.28 \times SCI \times 0.02$$
$$SCI = 0.223$$

Thus, the private automobile driver with a 22% risk of sustaining an SCI in the next year poses no greater threat to public safety than the heavy truck driver with a 1% risk.

Finally, for the commercial driver who drives a light vehicle, such as a taxicab or delivery truck, V = 0.28 and TD = 0.25, placing them at a risk between that of the private driver and the tractor-trailer driver.

References

1. Ostrom M, Eriksson A. Natural death while driving. *J Forensic Sci* 1987;32:988-98.
2. Hossack DW. Death at the wheel. A consideration of cardiovascular disease as a contributory factor to road accidents. *Med J Aust* 1974;I:164-6.
3. Parsons M. Fits and other causes of loss of consciousness while driving. *Q J Med* 1986;58:295-303.
4. Antecol DH, Roberts WC. Sudden death behind the wheel from natural disease in drivers of four wheeled motor vehicles. *Am J Cardiol* 1990;66:1329-35.
5. Ontario Ministry of Transportation. *1987 Ontario road safety annual report.* Toronto: Ministry of Transportation; 1987.
6. *Fuel consumption survey annual report:* October 1981 to September 1982 and October 1982 to September 1983. Ottawa: Statistics Canada; 1987. (Cat. no. 53-226)

Appendix G
DSM-IV* criteria for
substance abuse and dependence

Criteria for substance abuse

A. A maladaptive pattern of substance use leading to clinically significant impairment or distress, as manifested by 1 (or more) of the following, occurring within a 12-month period:
   1. recurrent substance use resulting in a failure to fulfill major role obligations at work, school or home (e.g., repeated absences or poor work performance related to substance use; substance-related absences, suspensions or expulsions from school; neglect of children or household)
   2. recurrent substance use in situations in which it is physically hazardous (e.g., driving an automobile or operating a machine when impaired by substance use)
   3. recurrent substance-related legal problems (e.g., arrests for substance-related disorderly conduct)
   4. continued substance use despite having persistent or recurrent social or interpersonal problems caused or exacerbated by the effects of the substance (e.g., arguments with spouse about consequences of intoxication, physical fights)
B. The symptoms have never met the criteria for substance dependence for this class of substance.

Criteria for substance dependence†

A maladaptive pattern of substance use, leading to clinically significant impairment or distress, as manifested by three (or more) of the following, occurring at any time in the same 12-month period:
1. tolerance, as defined by either of the following:
   a. a need for markedly increased amounts of the substance to achieve intoxication or desired effect

---

*Reprinted with permission from the *Diagnostic and Statistical Manual of Mental Disorders*, fourth edition. Washington: American Psychiatric Association; 1994.
†The DSM-IV classification of substance dependence includes further detail on classification of remission. The definitions of various types of remissions are based on the time interval that has elapsed since engagement in treatment and cessation of dependence. Remission is deemed possible after no criteria for dependence or abuse have been met for at least 1 month but it is recognized that during the first 12 months there is a higher risk for relapse. For further information please refer to DSM-IV.

   b.   markedly diminished effect with continued use of the same amount of the substance

2.   withdrawal, as manifested by either of the following:

   a.   the characteristic withdrawal syndrome for the substance (refer to criteria A and B of the criteria sets for Withdrawal from the specific substances)

   b.   the same (or a closely related) substance is taken to relieve or avoid withdrawal symptoms

3.   the substance is often taken in larger amounts or over a longer period than was intended

4.   there is a persistent desire or unsuccessful efforts to cut down or control substance use

5.   a great deal of time is spent in activities necessary to obtain the substance (e.g., visiting multiple doctors or driving long distances), use the substance (e.g., chain-smoking), or recover from its effects

6.   important social, occupational, or recreational activities are given up or reduced because of substance use

7.   the substance use if continued despite knowledge of having a persistent or recurrent physical or psychological problem that is likely to have been caused or exacerbated by the substance (e.g., current cocaine use despite recognition of cocaine-induced depression, or continued drinking despite recognition that an ulcer was made worse by alcohol consumption)

Specify if

•   with physiological dependence: evidence of tolerance or withdrawal (i.e., either item 1 or 2 is present)

•   without physiological dependence: no evidence of tolerance or withdrawal (i.e., neither item 1 nor 2 is present).

Reference Web sites

American Medical Association. *Physician's guide to assessing and counseling older drivers.* nhtsa.com/people/injury/olddrive/physician_guide/PhysiciansGuide.pdf

Austroads. Assessing fitness to drive: for commercial and private vehicle drivers, Australia. www.austroads.com.au/upload_files/docs/AFTD%202003-F_A-WEBREV1.pdf

British Columbia Medical Association, Emergency Medical Services Committee www.drivesafe.com

Canadian Cardiovascular Society. *Assessment of the cardiac patient for fitness to drive and fly: final report.* www.ccs.ca/download/consensus_conference/consensus_conference_archives/2003_Fitness.pdf

Canadian Diabetes Association's clinical practice guidelines for diabetes and private and commercial driving. *Can J Diabetes* 2003; 27(2):128-140. www.diabetes.ca/Files/Driving Guidelines.pdf

Canadian Diabetes Association 2003 clinical practice guidelines for the prevention and management of diabetes in Canada. *Can J Diabetes* 2003; 27(suppl. 2). www.diabetes.ca/cpg2003/downloads/cpgcomplete.pdf

CanDRIVE — Issues relating to older drivers. www.CanDRIVE.ca

Centers for Disease Control and Prevention. Impaired driving fact sheet. www.cdc.gov/ncipc/factsheets/drving.htm

Centers for Disease Control and Prevention. Quick facts about drunk and drugged driving. www.cdc.gov/ncipc/duip/spotlite/3d.htm

Dementia Network of Ottawa-Carleton and the Regional Geriatric Assessment Program. Driving and Dementia Toolkit. www.rgaottawa.com/dementia/rationale_en.asp

Driver and Vehicle Licensing Agency, UK. www.dvla.gov.uk

European Commission on Transport and Road Safety. Fitness to drive. ec.europa.eu /transport/roadsafety/behavior/fitness_to_drive_en.htm

Georgia Perimeter College. Global assessment of functioning (GAF) scale, abbreviated, without examples. www.gpc.edu/~bbrown/psyc2621/ch3/gaf.htm

International Commission for Driver Testing. *MEDRIL workshop report: practical fitness-to-drive assessments: on-road testing*. Belgium; 2005. www.cieca.be/download/MEDRIL MintesWS1.pdf

International Journal of Psychosocial Rehabilitation. Functional assessment of mental health and addiction scale. www.psychosocial.com/dualdx/famha.pdf

Monash University, Australia. *Influence of chronic illness on crash involvement of motor vehicle drivers*. www.monash.edu.au/muarc/reports/muarc213.html

National Institute on Alcohol Abuse and Alcoholism (NIAAA). *Helping patients who drink too much: a clinician's guide* (2005 ed.). pubs.niaaa.nih.gov/publications/Practitioner /CliniciansGuide2005/guide.pdf

Northern Health. *Crossroads: report on motor vehicle crashes in northern BC*; 2005. www.northernhealth.ca/News_Events/Media_Centre_and_News/documents /Crossroadsreport.pdf

Railway Association of Canada. *Canadian railway medical rules handbook*. www.railcan.ca /documents/circulars/657/2004_11_01_CMR_Handbook_en.pdf

Supreme Court of Canada. Grismer decision. scc.lexum.umontreal.ca/en/1999 /1999rcs3-868/1999rcs3-868.html

Traffic Research Laboratory, UK. Reports on traffic and road safety. www.trl.co.uk/store/report_list.asp?pid=108

Transport Canada, Civil Aviation Medicine Branch. www.tc.gc.ca/CivilAviation/Cam/

Transport Canada. *Handbook for civil aviation medical examiners*. www.tc.gc.ca/CivilAviation/Cam/tp13312-2/menu.htm

World Health Organization. AUDIT — *Alcohol use disorders identification test*. whqlibdoc.who.int/hq/2001/WHO_MSD_MSB_01.6a.pdf

Index

Note: References are to sections and subsections except where otherwise indicated.

truck drivers, 1.7, 1.10
Tumarkin's attacks, 12.3.2
tumour
    adrenal, 17.8.3
    brain, 10.5
    effects on driving, 20.2
    in pilots, 24.17
    intracranial, 10.8
    pituitary, 17.7.2
    spinal cord, 10.5

United States
    licensing, 1.3
    medical standards for driving,
    1.3

valvular heart disease, 13.5
    in pilots, 24.8.2
vascular diseases
    arterial aneurysm, 15.2
    diseases of the veins, 15.4
    effects on driving, 15.1

in pilots, 24.10
    peripheral arterial diseases, 15.3
vehicles
    classes, 1.10
    differing requirements, 1.7, 1.10
    modified for disability, 19.2.4,
    2.5
venous thrombosis, 15.4
    in pilots, 24.9
ventricular dysfunction, 13.6
    in pilots, 24.8.4
ventricular fibrillation, 13.3.1
ventricular tachycardia, 13.3.1
vertigo, 12.3.2
vestibular disorders, 12.3
    in pilots, 24.7, 24.11
VIA Rail Canada, 25.8
vision
    aids, *page* 50
    and pilots, 24.6
    colour, 11.3.1
    contrast sensitivity, 11.3.2

dark adaptation, 11.3.4
depth perception, 11.3.3
double, 11.2.3
effects on driving, 11.1
exceptional cases, 11.4
glare recovery, 11.3.4
night driving, 11.3.4
recommended standards, 11.2
testing procedures, *pages*48-50
visual acuity, 11.2.1
visual field, 11.2.2
    and pilots, 24.6

women, voluntary driving cessation,
    4.2

yardpersons (railway), 25.1, 25.6
Yukon
    Civil Aviation Medicine contact,
    24.20
    reporting contact, *page* 121
    reporting requirements, 3.2

Notes

Notes

Notes

Notes

Notes

Notes